SURVIVAL GUIDE

FOR THE ADMINISTRATIVE ASSISTANT

The complete guide
for successful office management

Justa Victorin

Amerista, LLC
Pembroke Pines, Florida

Library of Congress Cataloging-in-Publication number pending

Title: Survival Guide for the Administrative Assistant

ISBN 978-0-615-17619-2

For information to place an order, contact:

Amerista at (954) 579-2641

or visit us at

www.myofficecommunity.com

Email: JustaVictorin@aol.com

Contents

Appendix – Forms

Foreword

This book almost never got published, it was written back in 1999. That was before the Internet changed our lives. I looked at it a few times through the years. However, my vertigo made it impossible for me to continue the project.

I am an entrepreneur at heart, I used to watch The Apprentice. Donny Deutsch appeared in one of the first episodes and caught my attention. When he got his own show, I watched it sometimes but mostly because he wore the best business-casual clothes on TV. Then his show became a platform for entrepreneurs to share their experiences, I was hooked.

In July, Donny had a show about the possibility of an idea hiding in your attic that could be worth millions. I knew there was nothing in my attic. However, on a floppy, there was this book I started back in 1999. That show inspired me to finalize the book. I finished it and I am dedicating this book to Donny and to all those who share their stories on the Big Idea to inspire me.

Cheers to you,
Justa

Preface

The goal of this book is to share what I have learned through the years and create a contemporary methodology for the Administrative Assistant profession. I looked at the other books on the market and there was nothing like this book. It represents today's Administrative Assistant's work life; with its rewards and challenges.

My first wish is to bring to this profession the level of respect it deserves. People sometimes refer to this job as if it was very easy and a sub-class profession. The reality is that although you don't need a degree for this career, it still requires a certain amount of administrative knowledge. It is a white-collar job. To be a good Administrative Assistant, you have to be organized, knowledgeable and smart to fulfill the requirements of the job. The computer skills enough make you an expert.

My second wish is to become the "go to" person when an Administrative Assistant needs advice and to open a forum for professional discussion. Go to the website: www.myofficecommunity.com to join our community and share your experiences.

I want to thank my family for putting up with me while completing this book and all my friends for their support.

CHAPTER 1

INTRODUCTION: HISTORICAL PERSPECTIVE OF THE PROFESSION

The objective of this chapter is to provide the reader with a historical perspective and the opportunities of the profession.

The Administrative Assistant profession is one of the oldest professions in history. In the beginning, it was referred to as a secretary, which comes from the Latin word "secretarius" meaning one entrusted with secrets: a reminder of the amount of confidential information handled by the secretary. According to the Wikipedia encyclopedia, a "secretarius" was a person, overseeing business confidentially, usually for a powerful individual (a king, pope, etc.)

When looking at the logistics of the Administrative Assistant, the first thing that comes to mind is that men, since they were the ones in power, recreated the role of the spouse into the workplace. However, things have changed and the role of the former secretary was transformed to represent the new perception of the Administrative Assistant position in the workplace.

Have you ever entered a department without an Administrative Assistant? It's like entering a war zone without an army. A department without an Administrative Assistant is like a house without a caretaker, without a soul, without a heart, and let's not forget, unorganized. You are bound to find: faxes not distributed, paper piled in no specific order, messy desks, etc. I usually say that if management is the head of the company, the Administrative Assistant is the heart.

The Administrative Assistant's role reinvented

Many factors have contributed to the evolution of the Administrative Assistant's position. As technology became available, the expectation was that the need for secretaries would decline. Instead, the profession has created more demand, even evolving in two levels clearly defined as "Administrative Assistant" and "Executive Administrative Assistant." Because technology raised the productivity of the Administrative Assistant, the responsibilities have also evolved. It has provided the Administrative Assistant with a more diversified position leading to a pseudo-managing role.

As the workers' level of education improved, so did the profession. And as the companies downsized their middle managers, the assistants gained more responsibilities within the corporation. Today, the Administrative Assistant's role is one of decision-making in conjunction with the director or manager. The relationship between the manager and the assistant is of great importance. It's a very significant team with a special alliance.

The position is also used as an entry by young executives in search of a chance at having a foot in the door. They feel that if they are already on staff they can have a chance at internal promotions and eventually become managers.

The salaries also reflect the distinction in the titles. The salary for a Secretary is usually under $30,000 per year. According to www.payscale.com, the salary for the Administrative Assistant ranges from $35,282 for under a year of experience to over $48,000 per year for twenty years of experience or more. However, some executive Administrativc Assistants earn up to six-figure salaries when reporting to CEO's in big corporations. The best paying city for this job is San Francisco, earning $57,460 per year. The position is considered among the professions that earn the most money without a university degree and is still mainly held by women. It is also a career that makes you very employable. Every company needs an assistant.

Where are the work opportunities for an Administrative Assistant?

If you surf the web or check local newspapers, you will find that this position is needed in any company. Almost every business requires a good Administrative Assistant: from the car dealership to the insurance company. There are, however, some opportunities for Administrative Assistants to specialize in various fields.

Medical Assistant: this may require some additional training to become knowledgeable of the medical terminology. You can work for:

- Hospitals
- Health care organizations
- Physicians' offices
- Clinics

Your duties will include:

- Transcribing
- Minor billing
- Scheduling patients
- Confirming appointments
- Communicating with laboratories, Pharmaceutical companies and Pharmacies.

Legal Assistant: the Legal Assistant is one of the best paid in the profession. If a Legal Assistant is very experienced, he/she can be very well rewarded. The position requires:

- Client contact, scheduling and assisting
- Reviewing and editing of legal documents
- Keeping attorneys' schedules
- Scheduling court appearances and confirming clients' court dates.

Marketing Assistant: requires the assistant to:

- Communicate with advertising agencies, printers and advertising/promotional material manufacturers
- Ensure deadlines are met
- Coordinate departmental activities.

Accounting Assistant: for this field, it is important that the Administrative Assistant:

- Possesses advance knowledge in all Excel functions
- Is familiar with income tax returns.

Several schools offer income tax classes. The most popular is H&R Block. Check their site for prices and schedules at www.hrblock.com.

Celebrity Assistant: this is an emerging field that requires more Administrative Assistants. It is a great opportunity for an assistant to earn above average income. The job's financial rewards reflect the hectic schedule. The hours are not the nine-to-five norm. It's more a 24/7 broken down into sections. Personal assistants are required to do more than administrative functions. Their job description is more inclined towards personal work than administrative work. They sometimes work at the boss' house instead of an office. Some become famous by association with their bosses. P. Diddy a.k.a. Sean Combs recently hired an attorney to become his assistant through youtube.com. As a celebrity assistant, you may be required to:

- Organize the daily life of the celebrity
- Maintain their schedule
- Organize parties and events
- Coordinate travel, etc.

Inspirational Quote
"To love what you do and feel that it matters --how could anything be more fun?"
Catherine Graham

NOTES

CHAPTER 2

SURVIVING IN THE CORPORATION

In this chapter, various tips and insights are offered to help the Administrative Assistant survive in the corporation.

Working hard always pays. However, there are skills other than the administrative skills that are extremely important to be an effective Administrative Assistant; who will earn the respect of peers, colleagues and management. They are:

- **Adaptability:** your capacity to adapt quickly to a new environment or the culture of a company. Working today is like a marriage. The key to a successful partnership requires some compromising and your adaptability to changes in the corporation.

- **Ability to meet deadlines:** the nine-to-five jobs are no longer here. They are a thing of the past. As today's worker juggles many hats, it becomes harder to meet the deadlines. However, your ability to meet deadlines is vital to your survival. Your reputation, your integrity and your professionalism are at risk. You must meet your deadlines. When you promise to have an assignment ready for a certain date, make sure that you deliver. If for any reason you are unable to meet a deadline, request for a revised date and inform the party waiting for the job. This is, however, a last resort move.

- **Be consistent:** one of the best ways to gain respect and have a good reputation is to be consistent. Do exactly what you said you would do, how you said you would do it, when you said you would do it and the way you said you would do it. Be someone who is accountable and the best resource of your company. Someone they can count on. By following these guidelines, you will become the "go to" person and someone who is respected.

- **Use of good judgment:** always consult your boss before making decisions that concern him/her. You work for decision makers, you are bound to bear some of the responsibilities. Your role puts you in a position of diplomacy, tact, judgment and discretion. You are the glue of your department, the organizer, the planner, the scheduler, the arranger and the problem-solver. You must be discrete, mature, in control and tactful.

- **Networking:** you must have the ability to build relationships at all levels inside and outside the company. Therefore, your capacity to network, or make contacts in the workplace, is a survival skill that is as important as your academic knowledge base. As technology makes us lose the personal touch, it becomes even more important to make contacts. In the corporate world where downsizing is a process of eliminating the unwanted and the undesired, your ability to communicate and network is considered survival-like skills. If you build a good and solid reputation, it's hard for anyone to destroy your reputation. You will also be last to go should your company decide to downsize.

- **Diplomatic:** you must be diplomatic in your dealings with your co-workers. Remember it's your reputation and your boss' reputation that are at stake. In today's business world, your people skills are very important. Your ability to deal effectively with co-workers is your greatest asset.

Inspirational Quote
"When one door of happiness closes, another opens; but often we look so long at the closed door that we do not see the one which has opened for us."
--Helen Keller

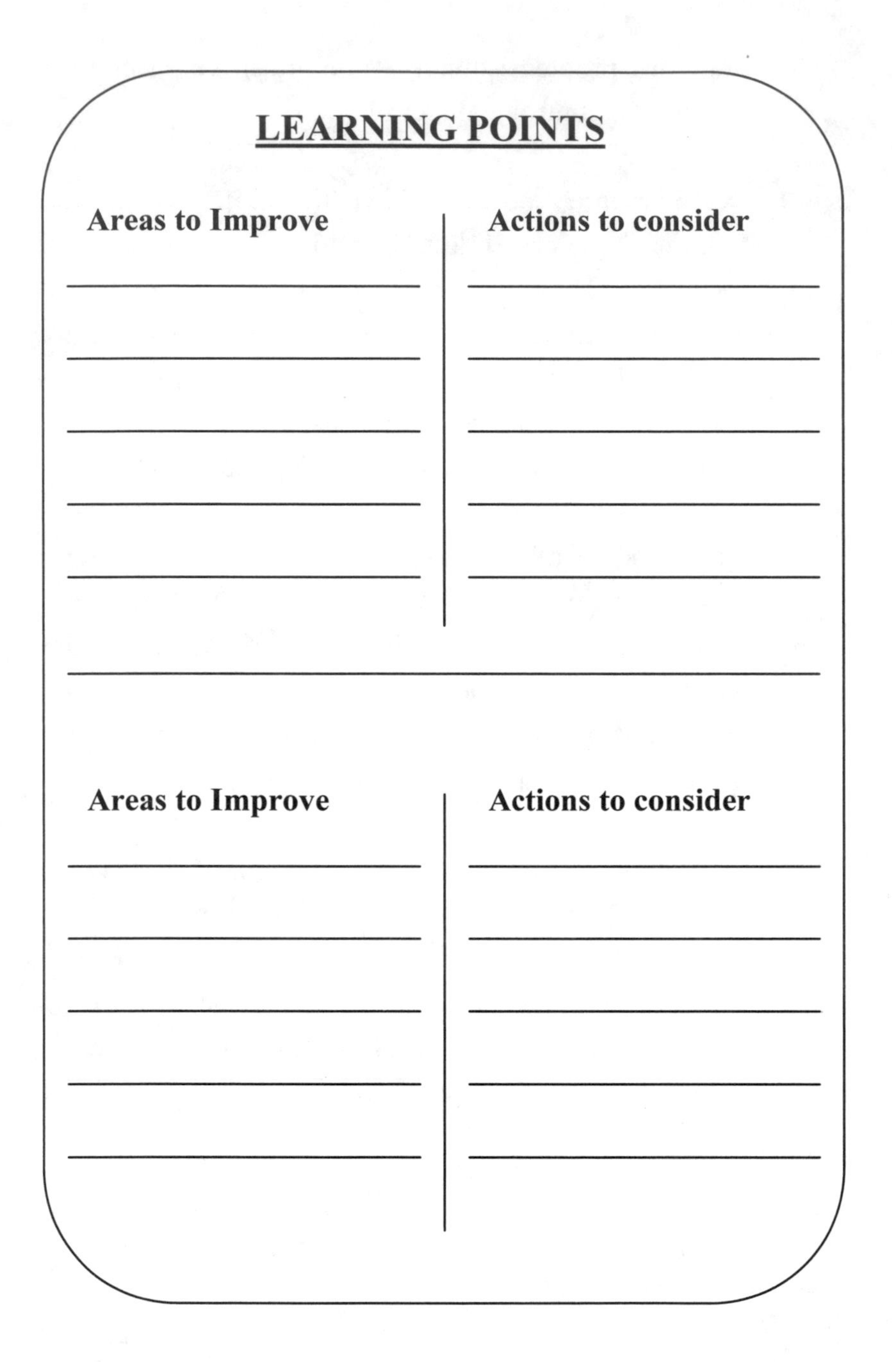
LEARNING POINTS
Areas to Improve
Actions to consider
Areas to Improve
Actions to consider

What I learned from this chapter:

NOTES

CHAPTER 3

GETTING ORGANIZED

This chapter provides Management and Administrative Assistants with the tools and systems to get organized, prepare for emergencies and general office filing rules and regulations. It also offers guidelines to create a job description for the administrative position or other positions as required by management.

- Time management
- Preparing a job description
- Organizing your files
- Create an emergency plan and contacts.

Time Management

One of our most important resources is also the most volatile: "time." Once gone, you can't recapture it. One must to use it wisely and effectively. Time management is multifaceted and includes a variety of activities from managing, scheduling, planning, prioritizing and organizing. Managing time can also be time consuming.

Managing your time requires planning your work, your life and sometimes, your boss' life. As an assistant, it is difficult to effectively manage your time since you work based on what your boss wants you to execute. However, if there are other areas of your job that do not require the involvement of your boss, it is recommended that those activities be scheduled effectively.

Planning: create a plan to organize yourself. The plan will include your goals based on your boss' plan, both short-term and long-term. Planning allows for better workflow and provides direction. When planning, remember to set deadlines for yourself and/or your projects. Planning will keep you focused, disciplined and organized. If you plan, you won't procrastinate.

Scheduling: use electronic systems to manage your schedule. If you don't have electronic systems, put your appointments on paper calendar/planner. Whatever system you choose, you must be consistent. You need to have the tools to serve as reminders. It's the best way to be organized and maintain a schedule. One of the greatest tools to use when scheduling while in the office is Microsoft Outlook and when out, there are various PDA's (Personal Digital Assistants) and phones that allow you to schedule your work. If you can use these systems simultaneously, they will keep you organized. Outlook is reviewed in the technology section of this book.

One of the most innovative functions of the systems, such as Outlook and the PDA's is their ability to communicate with each other through synchronization. You can install software on your computer that will communicate with your PDA or phone. This means that the information you schedule in the office and outside of the office is merged and updated into both systems.

Using Outlook, or the other systems, you can enter appointments, tasks, meetings and events. You can also insert notes and specifics of the appointment, task or meeting. If you plan your work well, you will feel less rushed and less stressed. It's important to have good systems in place that will not fail you by not reminding you of your scheduled appointments.

Prioritizing: prioritizing your work is a very important aspect of time management. It allows for proper allocation of time to various projects by order of importance. It will enable you to work on the important projects first and the less important ones later.

Things to do: in order to avoid wasting time, always have a "to do list." Prioritize the list by order of importance of the task or by time slots. Execute the most important items first and finish the last item at the end. You can, however, set aside time to perform specific tasks. This is most effective if you have tasks that can be scheduled. For instance, if you must file documents, perhaps set aside time weekly to attend to your filing duties.

Time and the telephone: one of the most time consuming aspects of your job is attending the phone. A lot of people recommend that you let all your calls go to voicemail and establish certain time slots to answer or listen to your messages. Your job is too important not to attend the phone. You are the link to most departments or people in your company. It is strongly recommended that you answer your phone at all times and by the third ring. You want to be consistent in the way you deal with answering the phone.

Overall, being organized will make you a more efficient, effective and valuable asset. Your boss will feel that you are a dependable and trustworthy employee.

If you work for a small company that does not have the resources to afford a PDA, you can use a small calendar or a small wire-bound notebook. The advantage of using them is that you have everything on paper. However, they won't remind you of your appointments unless you look at them. The technological tools have the benefit of ringing bells and catching your attention through pop up messages. Your cell phone may come in handy to schedule with a buzzer when you don't have a PDA.

Another way of staying organized is by keeping things in their place. This will avoid wasting time looking for misplaced or misfiled documents. This can be a great source of lost time.

Negative factors affecting your time management:

- Unwanted interruptions
- Chatty co-workers
- Procrastination
- The telephone
- Cluttered workspace
- Misfiling and misplacing documents or anything you need for your work.

Organizing your files

The organization of department files is extremely important to your company. Therefore, you should make due diligence to ensure that the files are well maintained and that, depending on the industry you work for, the amount of time a file must be kept is followed. Medical, legal, real estate, schools, etc., have some specific requirements as to the number of years the files must be kept. Some companies, if their filing capacity is maximized and the length of time they are required to maintain their files is not expired, outsource their filing to an outside filing or data storage company. There is a whole industry dedicated to managing files for their clients. Remember to destroy files that have expired. This will free up filing space.

Enclosed is a list of guidelines to set up a filing system:

Administrative:
- Office information
- Meetings

Financial:
- Accounts Receivables
- Expense reports
- Invoices

Personnel:

- Current Employee files
- Terminated employee files
- Payroll
- Timesheets
- Vacation

Vendors:

- Accounts Payable
- Vendor files
- Product information
- Catalogs

Sales and Marketing:

- Customers
- Prospects
- Brochures
- Newsletters
- Competitors information/documentation
- Surveys
- List of products/services
- Price lists
- Customer service reviews.

Preparing a Job Description

If your company does not have a job description for your position, you should create one. If there is one and your job requires more than what is determined by your job description, you need to update your job description.

Your job description is simply a summary of your daily, weekly and monthly activities divided into specific categories. Ever wonder where the day has gone? A good way to monitor how time is spent is to document the time consumed on your daily activities. Enclosed is a grid that can be used to tally your activities.

ACTIVITY	QTY	TIME
Number of calls received		
Number of calls made		
Number of messages taken		
Letters/documents typed		
Photocopies		
Meetings scheduled		
Meeting attended (duration)		
Data entry or other typing		
Binding		
Report typing		
Order taking		
Document reviewing		

A job description should be as detailed as possible. It is a detailed outline of the work you perform as an employee and the responsibilities assigned to you or that you have taken the initiative for. If you are performing duties on a temporary basis, remember to add a section to include those duties. Do not hesitate to segment your job description. It is rccommended that you have both a general job description and/or a partial job description. A condensed version of your job description will eventually become your resume.

Keep track of the hours you work even if you are an exempt employee. Being an exempt employee means that you are not entitled to be paid overtime. When documenting the number of hours you work, you should enter the real times that you come in and leave, even if you are unable to claim those overtime hours. This is a good way of protecting yourself should you need some time off and are refused. All these components will be used to document the work you perform, and ultimately, to write your job description.

Emergency Planning and First Aid

Having an emergency plan is important and vital to the survival and continuity of the organization. The first reason is to help the employees if the emergency is life threatening. The second is to enable the company to keep operating as usual. To help plan for emergencies, offices should keep an emergency plan containing: a) contact information about the responsible parties, including who does what and their contact information; b) information and items to be kept to maintain the viability of the company during and after the emergency.

FEMA recommends the following action items to protect business records and inventory

Protecting your business from natural disasters can involve a variety of actions, from inspecting and maintaining your buildings to installing protective devices. Most of these actions, especially those that affect the structure of your buildings or their utility systems, should be carried out by qualified maintenance staff or professional contractors licensed to work in your state, county, or city. One example of disaster protection is safely storing the important documents, electronic files, raw materials, and inventory required for the operation of your business.

Protect business records and inventory

Most businesses keep off-site records and files (both hardcopy and electronic) that are essential to normal operations. Some businesses also store raw materials and product inventory. The loss of essential records, files, and other materials during a disaster is commonplace and can not only add to your damage costs, but also delay your return to normal operations. The longer the business is not operating, the more likely it is to lose customers permanently to its competitors.

To reduce vulnerability, determine which records, files, and materials are most important. Consider their vulnerability to damage during different types of disasters, such as floods, hurricanes, and earthquakes; and take steps to protect them, including the following:

- Raising computers above the flood level and moving them away from large windows
- Moving heavy and fragile object to low shelves
- Storing vital documents (plans, legal papers, etc.) in a secure off-site location
- Regularly backing up vital electronic files (such as billing, payroll records and customer lists) and storing backup copies in a secure off-site location.
- Securing equipment that could move or fall during an earthquake.

Tips

Keep these points in mind when protecting business records and inventory:

- Make sure you know the details of the flood insurance and other hazard insurance policies, specifically which items and contents are covered and under what conditions. For example, if you work for a home-based business, two flood insurance policies may be needed, a home policy and a separate business policy, depending on the percentage of the total square footage of the house that is devoted to business use.

Check with the insurance agent if there are questions about any of the policies

- When you identify equipment that is susceptible to damage, consider the location of the equipment. For example, equipment near a hot water tank or pipes could be damaged if the pipes burst during an earthquake, and equipment near large windows could be damaged during hurricanes
- Disaster mitigation duties should be assigned to employees. For example, some employees could be responsible for securing storage bins and others for backing up computer files and delivering copies to a secure location
- You may want to suggest having other offices in the company, or a contractor, perform some administrative duties, such as maintaining payroll records or providing customer service
- Estimate the cost of repairing or replacing each essential piece of equipment in the company. The estimates will help assess vulnerability and focus the efforts where required
- For both insurance and tax purposes, written and photographic inventories of all important materials and equipment should be maintained. The inventory should be stored in a safety deposit box or other secure location.

MANAGING YOUR INFORMATION TECHNOLOGY IN TIME OF CRISIS

In today's computerized world, IT data and equipment are vital to the survival and continuation of a business. Depending on the size of the company, a person or a team of IT employees should be assigned as primary contact persons responsible for maintaining the company data safely; stored off-site and readily available in case of emergency. If only one person is assigned, have a secondary back-up contact should the first responsible person not bc available or sick.

Employees are encouraged to:

- Store their data files on CD's, flash drives, etc. so they can access them off-site in case of an emergency.

- Create a secondary email account on one of the free email provider sites such as: Yahoo, Gmail, AOL or Hotmail. If your company email is down, you can use one of them. You should also keep a copy of your address book in this secondary email address. It will come in handy should you need to use that account.

EMERGENCY PREPARATION AND INFORMATION	
Contact Information	• Names and contact information of company officers. • Preferably their cell or home phone numbers.
Medical Information	• Names of employees who have taken CPR and can administer first aid if needed • Contact information for nearest hospital.
General Items	• Petty cash, if needed • Flashlights and batteries • Battery-operated radio and/or TV • Whistle • Fire extinguisher • Matches or lighters • Portable fans or heater • Clean-up solvent • Camera or camera recorder to document damage • Blankets and covers.

First Aid Kit	• Sterile adhesive bandages
	• Latex gloves
	• Compresses
	• Non-prescription medicines:
	  • Pain reliever
	  • Antiseptic
	  • Antacid, nausea, stomach
	  • Anti-diarrhea medication.

Food and Drink	• Drinking water • Coolers for food and drinks • Ice • Canned drinks and sodas • Ready to eat canned meats, fruits and vegetables.

In states or countries where natural disasters occur frequently, companies have taken steps to make their businesses disaster-ready by installing generators and other equipment that will enable them to continue their operations throughout the local disaster. Disasters are local in nature so if the company is national or global, it needs to remain open to serve its customers.

NATIONAL EMERGENCY CONTACTS	
FEMA - Federal Emergency Management Agency www.fema.gov	1-800-621-3362
Mail Services	1-800-275-8777
Social Security Administration	1-800-772-1213
Attorney General's Price Gouging Hotline	1-800-646-0444
American Red Cross Redcross.org	1-800-435-7669
Salvation Army Donations Helpline www.salvationarmy.org	1-800-275-2769
American Red Cross Food, Shelter and Financial Assistance www.redcross.org	1-866-438-4636
National Oceanic and Atmospheric Administration – noaa.gov	1-202-482-6090

Inspirational Quote

"Plan your work for today and every day, then work your plan".- Norman Vincent Peale

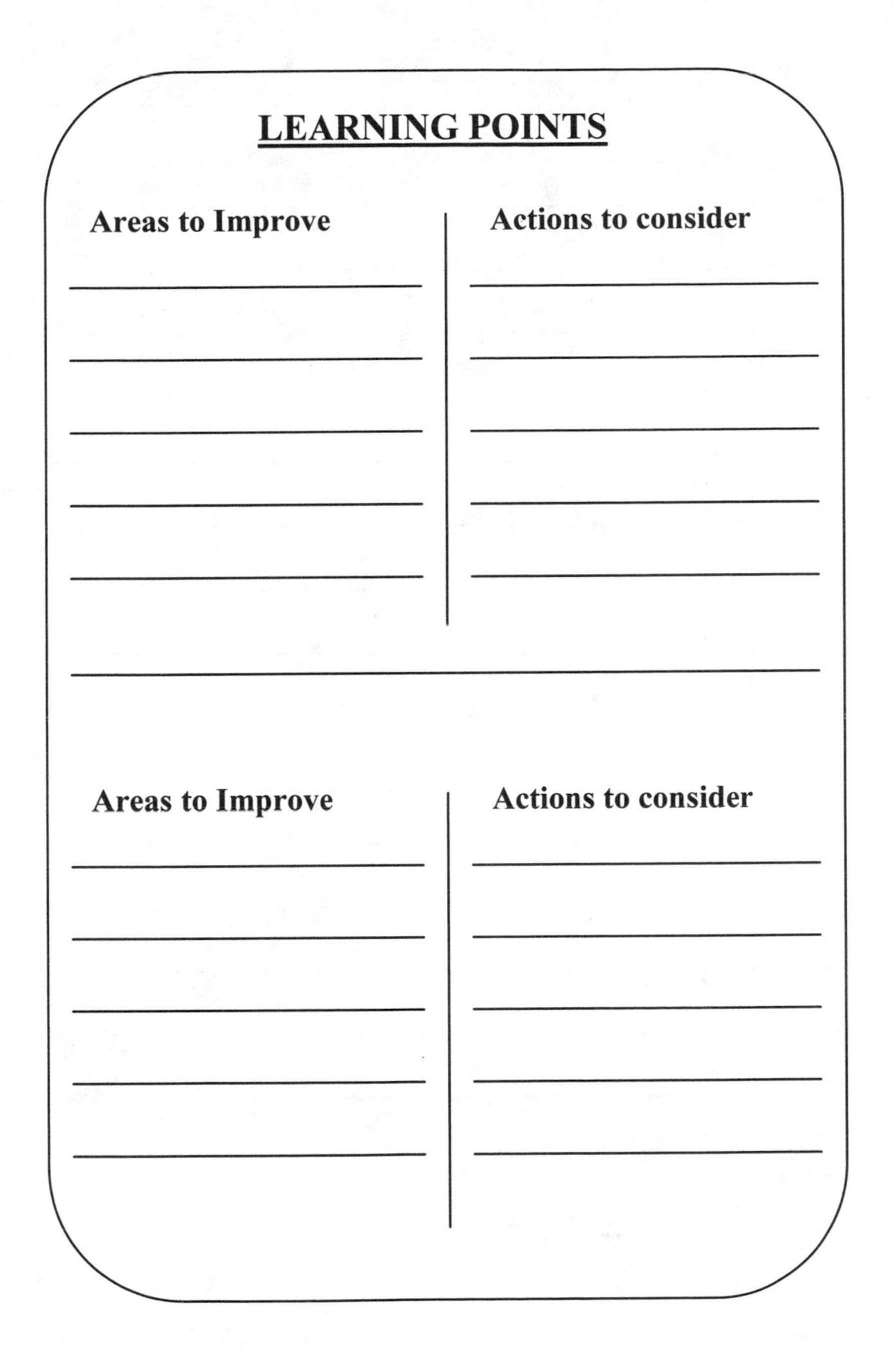
LEARNING POINTS
Areas to Improve
Actions to consider
Areas to Improve
Actions to consider

What I learned from this chapter:

NOTES

CHAPTER 4

MEETING, CONFERENCE AND EVENT PLANNING

This section of the book can be used by numerous professions. It is intended as a guide for the Administrative Assistant to prepare the meeting and assist a manager, meeting leader, or anyone who conducts an event or a meeting. However, others including but not limited to, conference/event planners and party planners can benefit from these guidelines, as well.

Meeting, Conference and Event Planning – How to organize a meeting or an event

- Purpose of the meeting - Planning the meeting
- Attendance, location, date and time
- The meeting notice
- The agenda: Items of discussion
- The sign-in sheet
- Making the reservations for meeting room and food
- Final preparations for the meeting
- The meeting minutes
- Distributing the meeting minutes
- Filing the meeting minutes.

How to Organize a Meeting

The success of a meeting is a direct reflection of its preparation. A successful meeting requires a substantial amount of planning and the organization of a meeting is a lengthy process that involves a lot of work.

I have recaptured all the "things to do" prior to holding a meeting. Since the purpose of meetings differ from corporation to corporation, from business to business and from department to department, the following guidelines can be customized to your specific department needs or to the needs of your organization. The same applies to planning an event and entertaining. This book can be customized to organize whatever meeting or event you are planning.

Purpose of the Meeting - Planning: Attendance, Location, Time and Date

The five "W's" of meeting organization:

1. **Why:** the first thing that you need to know is the purpose of the meeting. Every meeting has an objective. If there is a main purpose for the meeting it can be used in the heading, for example: "Customer Service Meeting." If the meeting is from a group or department, you can use the title of the group as the title of the meeting, i.e. "Engineering Department Meeting." The purpose of the meeting will provide the information for the agenda and materials (hand-outs) to be prepared for the meeting. Typically, the meeting leader will provide this information along with any other members participating in the meeting.

2. **Who:** who will participate and/or will be invited to the meeting? Once you find out the purpose of the meeting, inquire about the participants in the meeting. The next step is to create a list of the participants (those on the agenda) and guests (invited as speakers or as a courtesy.) That will be your distribution list.

3. **When:** now that you know the why of the meeting and who is attending, it's time to decide on the date, time and length of the meeting. You need to schedule a start and end time. It is important to stick to the schedule.

Once the list of participants is established, contact the guests and participants. Provide participants with alternate dates to choose from if you have a lot of time prior to the meeting. It is always recommended to schedule a meeting a month ahead of time.

4. **What:** what is the main item of discussion of the meeting? What will be the items on the agenda? If this is the first time the meeting is being conducted, the agenda will be built from scratch. The subsequent meeting agendas will be a continuation of the first agenda.

   If the meeting is departmental, the contributing members can provide you with their agenda items. These items of discussion will be on the agenda, as well as, those of guests who will be invited to the meeting to present their agenda items.

5. **Where:** once the date and time are determined, you need a place. The meeting location will reflect the number of participants. Your room must accommodate the number of participants and guests. The size of the meeting will determine whether you want to hold the meeting on-site or off-site. This is the most important part of the meeting, you must ensure that the location is reserved and confirmed. A written confirmation is always preferred as it will be your proof should the meeting room be double-booked. Imagine having a bunch of people all ready for a meeting and no place to

hold the meeting. It would be embarrassing. This is what will happen if the room is not confirmed.

Keep in mind that if the meeting has more participants than previously scheduled, you need the appropriate accommodations.

The Meeting Notice

Once the meeting date, time and location are established, send the meeting notice or invitations. The notice will be sent to all the participants. It is recommended that the notice include a request for items of discussion at the upcoming meeting.

The next Marketing meeting will be held on:
June 5, 2000
From: 9:00 a.m. to 12:00 p.m.
The meeting will take place at:
The Star Hotel, 200 N. E. 25th Avenue,
Somewhere Warm, CA 33333

The purpose of the meeting is to present the new marketing plan for the new Excelsior 2000. Please confirm your availability by contacting Mary Nelson at 555-6666. Also, remember to send your items of discussion for the agenda.

If the meeting was confirmed at the previous meeting, the notice can start with:

- As agreed at the last meeting
- As confirmed at the last meeting
- As scheduled at the last meeting.

Always include directions to the location of the meeting in the notice, along with a telephone number to contact if someone needs directions or can't find the meeting location.

Enclosed is a sample of a meeting notice:

MARKETING MEETING NOTICE

FROM: Marketing Director

DISTRIBUTION:
- Marketing Manager
- Marketing Coordinator
- CFO
- COO

The next Marketing meeting will be held on:
Date: June 5, 2000,
Time: 9:00 a.m. - 12:00 p.m.

The meeting will take place at:
The Star Hotel
200 N. E. 25th Avenue
Somewhere Warm, CA 33333.

The purpose of the meeting is to present the new marketing plan for the new Excelsior 2000. Please confirm your availability by contacting Mary Nelson at 555-555-5555. Also, remember to send your items of discussion for the agenda.

Include directions to the meeting.

The Agenda: Items of Discussion

Preparing the agenda:

The agenda should have the title of the meeting, the date, time and location of the meeting. If the group meeting is defined, the agenda should describe the group and include the group distribution list.

Previous agendas can be used as a guideline. Directors, managers and other interested parties will be providing agenda items to be included on the agenda via e-mail, by phone or in person. Keep the information in the meeting folder.

Send invitations to all participants. Request for a RSVP and keep a list of all those who confirm. If a participant has not replied, contact that person to request a confirmation of attendance.

Enclosed is a sample of an agenda

MARKETING MEETING

LOCATION: Conference Room - 3rd Floor
MEETING DATE: Thursday, September 06, 2007
TIME: 9:00 - 11:00 a.m.

DISTRIBUTION LIST:

Meeting Master
Marketing Manager
Marketing Coordinator
CFO
Engineering Manager

A G E N D A:

1. Minutes of the Meeting of (previous meeting date)
   1.1 Approve Minutes — Meeting Master
   1.2 Review Action Items — Meeting Master

2. Marketing Update — E-Commerce Manager
   2.1. Timelines — Marketing Coordinator
   2.2. Pay per Click — Marketing Coordinator
   2.3. Marketing Budget — CFO

3. Operations
   3.1. New Site Recommendation — Engineering Manager
   3.2. Site Cost Evaluation — CFO
   3.3. Site Construction — Engineering Manager

4. Finance

5. Production

6. Human Resources

7. Next Meeting Date

8. Meeting Adjournment

The Sign-In Sheet

To confirm attendance of the meeting participants, create a sign-in sheet. Include title, location, date and time of meeting. Put all the names, and leave enough space for signatures.

MARKETING MEETING SIGN-IN SHEET Thursday, September 06, 2007	
NAME	SIGNATURE
Meeting Master's Name	
Marketing Manager Name	
Marketing Coordinator Name	
CFO	
COO	
Engineering Manager	

Making the Reservations for Meeting Room and Food

Choosing a place for your meeting: do you have enough room to accommodate your guests on-site or will you go to a hotel or an off-site location for the meeting? Ensure that the hotel or place is centrally located for easy access to all the participants.

A few issues to address:

- Is the conference room big enough to accommodate all the participants?
- Does the hotel/meeting place have food service? If not, will they allow you to order in?
- Is there a telephone? Should there be any off-site employees who will join via teleconference
- Do you need audiovisual equipment? Does the location have them? Will the facility provide paper, pencil, water and drinks in the conference room?
- Reserve meeting room
- If off-site, reserve hotel rooms if needed
- Order lunch/dessert
- Drinks, cups, utensils, plates, napkins, water, etc.

The size of the meeting will determine the choice of a caterer or a restaurant for the meeting. Because most of caterers will charge a substantial amount per person, if the meeting is a small meeting, it is recommended that you order from a gourmet restaurant near the location of the meeting.

It's great to provide your guests a variety of quality restaurant grade food. Not everyone likes the same food. Therefore, when ordering, ensure that there is a variety of the main course, drinks and dessert.

Check list of items needed to cater a meeting:

- Food/sandwiches
- Dessert
- Plates
- Cups
- Utensils
- Napkins
- Drinks
- Juice
- Water
- Ice
- Coffee
- Toothpicks

Always order at least a few salads and a variety of salad dressings!

MEETING PREPARATION SHEET

Title of meeting:	
Meeting Owner:	
Location	
Confirmed: Yes ☐ by	
Room Capacity	
Number of participants	
Date of meeting	
Time of meeting	From: To:
Meeting notice sent	
2 days Prior to meeting, send last notice	
Caterer	
Telephone number	

Items required for the meeting

MEETING MATERIALS
• Agenda and attachments • Minutes of previous meeting • Sign-in sheet • Table tents, business cards • Equipment • Flip charts • Projector or overhead projector • Projector screen • High intensity overhead (can be used as a back-up) • Microphones • Extension cords • Computer and computer hook-ups • Internet access or wireless • Recorder, cassettes and batteries • Conference phone and phone extension cord • Office supplies: Pens, markers, masking tape, chart paper, etc.

Final Preparations for the Meeting

Enclosed are the final steps to prepare for the meeting. You have already prepared the agenda, sent the notice, confirmed the meeting room and prepared the menu. On the meeting preparation sheet found in the forms section (located in the back of book,) mark all the items that have been finalized. Enclosed is a short list of things to do:

- One day prior to the meeting, prepare a meeting packet for the meeting leader, including the agenda, the previous meeting minutes and the hand-outs. Have enough copies; for the meeting leader, for you and for all other participants
- Bring the meeting folder
- Remember to confirm the meeting location
- Send a last reminder via email to all participants
- Confirm with the caterer or restaurant
- Reserve all audio equipment
- Bring office supplies, if necessary.

Going to the meeting and setting up

Arrive at least one hour prior to the meeting to ensure that everything is prepared and that all equipment is functional.

The Meeting Minutes

Most meeting leaders will document their meetings and make their own report of the minutes. However, some companies require that the Administrative Assistant provides at least a draft of the meeting minutes. If you are in charge of taking the minutes, you need to provide them to all meeting attendees. On Microsoft.com you can find templates of meeting minutes to guide you if you have never drafted meeting minutes before.

A draft of the minutes should be forwarded to the meeting leader for his/her review within four days following the meeting. The corrections, if any, should be added to the minutes. When finalized, the updated version will be distributed as follows:

- Ask the meeting leader for additional parties who should have copies
- Fax or email the minutes to the meeting participants and the parties that were copied on the agenda and notice.

Keeping the minutes filed

- File the minutes in the appropriate filing place; including all pertinent documents distributed at the meeting attached
- A routing sheet for filing can be created to ensure proper filing of meeting documentation.

Enclosed is a cheat sheet for drafting minutes

Minutes – Cheat Sheet	
Adhere	Informed
Adherence	Inquire about
Advised	Interested
Agreed	Investigate the feasibility
Agreement	Issue, on the issue
Appointed	Mentioned
Appropriate	Necessary
Asked were	Noted
Assembled	Notified
Benefited	Outline
Commented	Overview, give an
Communicated	Participated
Concerning	Presented
Confirmed	Provided
Comprised	Regarding, with regards
Considered	Relayed
Decided	Reported
Describe	Represented
Desired	Requested
Determined	Require
Discussions regarding	Resolved
Concluded	Set-up
Emphasized	Settled
Encouraged	Subject to
Essential	Submitted
Expected	Suggested
Featured	Supplement
Given was	Unanimously
Identified	Updated
Implemented	Used
Indicated	

Inspirational Quote

"Failures are finger posts on the road to achievement."
--C. S. Lewis

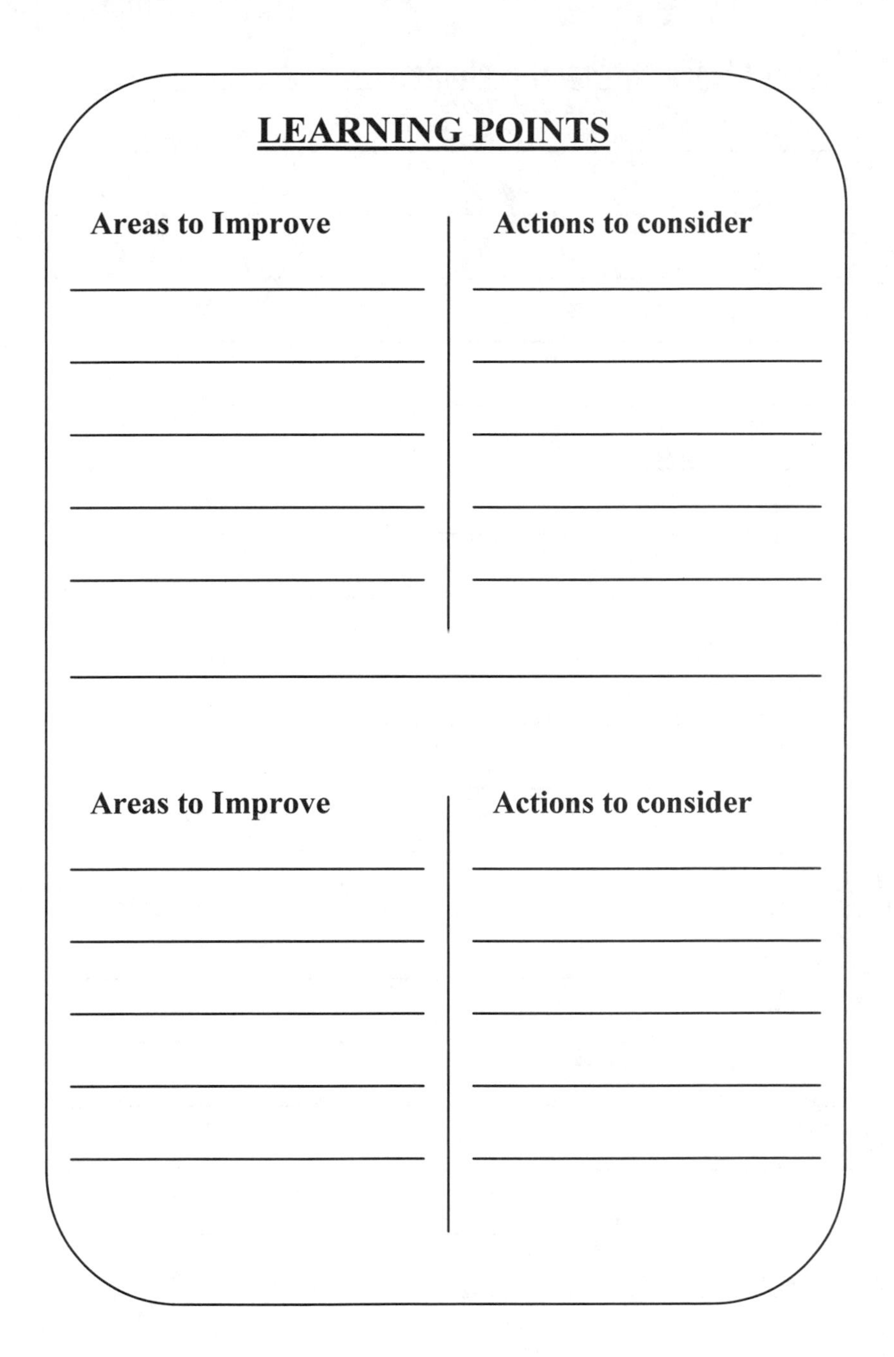
LEARNING POINTS
Areas to Improve
Actions to consider
Areas to Improve
Actions to consider

What I learned from this chapter:

NOTES

CHAPTER 5

CUSTOMER SERVICE

This chapter covers the very important subject of customer service for inside and outside clients.

Good Customer Service
=
Happy Customers and Profitable Company

Customer service may be referred to as: customer care, client services, client support, account management, account servicing, etc. Whatever the term used, it means that one must provide excellent service to your clients within a reasonable time frame and at an affordable cost.

One of the most important, if not the most important, roles of the professional Administrative Assistant is to provide quality customer service. That service is not limited to "outside" clients, but should be available to other departments as well, otherwise referred to as "inside" clients. Your position may not require you to deal with clients, but you need to offer courteous service to anyone who calls your department, your boss or anyone else in your group.

What is customer service? It can be defined as "do onto others as you would have them onto you." It's as simple as being courteous to a customer or co-worker. It is the process of providing proper service to a client. It should be a standard, but because of different ideas of how to offer service, companies have to provide training to their employees in order to ensure that clients are served with the required care or receive standardized assistance.

Tom Peters wrote a book in the 80's called: "In Search of Excellence." It is a must read for anyone who provides customer service for a living. Learning customer service that will wow your clients is extremely important.

What do customers want? Why is customer service so important? Depending on the occasion, customers want different things. However, like Oprah said, "The one thing everyone wants is to be validated." People want to know that they matter and their issues are important. If a customer is trying to find help to fix a product, that customer wants to know that the product can be fixed or replaced. A good example of how companies are providing excellent customer service is how customers can return any product purchased without question to the big stores like Wal-Mart, Target, Macy's, etc. Years ago, the consumer had to explain why they wanted to return or exchange a product.

We all know the saying: "It's not personal, it's business." With customer service, "it's personal, it's not business." However, the "personal" is not directed towards you the customer service representative. The client does not know you personally. It's directed to whoever is providing the service.

People want to be listened to when they have a problem. They want the employee to show:

- Empathy: show understanding and compassion towards someone's problem
- Sympathy: be caring and genuine
- Fairness: provide the same level of service to all
- Friendliness: the best customer service is to be friendly. The way you approach a customer has a big impact on the end result
- Important: customers want to feel that they are important and that you appreciate their business. They have choices. They could have picked another company; they chose "you"
- Appreciated: they don't want to be put down. They want to be treated with respect.

How do you provide the best customer service possible?

- One of the first qualities of customer service personnel should be that they enjoy working with people and helping others. If you are not a people person, you will need to adjust and learn how to be professional in providing customer service
- For instance, you are on the phone and an employee from another department comes to see you. Do you:

  a) ignore your visitor and continue on the phone
  b) acknowledge the person and continue with your phone conversation
  c) kindly ask the person on the phone to hold for a minute and find out what the person wants.

If you chose "c," you are a winner! You are an excellent customer service provider. There is nothing more frustrating than to wait for another person who is talking on the phone. After inquiring what the person needs, you can continue your conversation and attend the needs of that person later. It would become a problem if you left that person waiting while continuing your conversation on the phone.

Suggestions to handle an angry customer

A customer calls your department. He/she is angry because of multiple call transfers from department to department. You must stop all the call transfers and become the last person this client will talk to on that day and for this incident. The next steps taken should be:

- To listen attentively to the client's concerns and complaints
- Write key items carefully as client speaks
- When client is finished venting, ask for his/her name and telephone number in case you get disconnected
- Assure the client that you will not transfer him/her to another department and that you will find the information and return the call
- Review client concerns as written on your note
- Ensure that you understand correctly what the client's concern is
- Tell the client when you will call back. Give a specific time and ask if this time is suitable
- Research the problem and find a solution for this client
- Once you have completed your investigation and have a solution, call back client with

information/findings at the time promised. If for any reason, you don't find the information by the time agreed, make a courtesy call to advise client that you are still working to find the information and that you will call as soon as you find the information

- Should you not find the information on the same day, never go home without advising the client that you will call back tomorrow. Remember to apologize for the delay
- When you finish and find information, call the client
- Remember to conclude with a request to the client: "Are you satisfied with this information and if there is anything else I can do for you?"

Customer Service as a company's mission

A company's mission/vision is to provide its customers quality product/services at the best possible price. Customer service's role is to ensure that this vision is well perceived and the product/service is delivered professionally. Without customers, there is no company, no income, profits, business, period!

Customer service is the center of the company. It's the department where all the customers' requests come through and is the vehicle that will enable the company to customize services/products according to customers' needs and specifications. These requests are communicated to the various departments to ensure that proper attention is given to customers' requests and needs.

There are many ways of setting up customer service. The two models visited in this book are: unassigned clients suitable for a big call center and assigned clients when the level of care must be more personal. They are as follows:

a) The unassigned client model: Is suitable for a general call center in a big company (for instance a credit card company,) where the calls are channeled to the next available agent. The center serves all the customers by going through one telephone number channeled according to the sequence in which the calls are received. No intentional relationship is developed through that center. The customer calls and speaks to whoever answers the telephone. The weakness of this model is that relationship building is non-existent

b) The assigned customers' model is more suitable for a personalized service established by territory, alpha or numeric identification of the customer base. A company that may benefit with this arrangement is a small department that provides support to a sales force. In this model, each customer service representative would have his/her own base of clients. Each agent would have the full responsibility of receiving calls from his/her assigned customers. If the representative is unable to answer, the customers would have the choice of dialing 0 to be serviced by the next available customer service representative or to leave a voice mail message for his/her assigned agent. A recorded greeting will indicate that choice when the call goes to the agent's voice mail

- The assigned client base setting enables relationship building between customers and the customer service representatives. Building relationships is essential to doing business today. It is a very efficient way of maintaining customers' loyalty. People feel a sense of comfort when they know the person they are calling. They feel that can count and rely on a specific person

- The customer service rep dedicated to specific accounts allows for relationship continuity and knowledge of account activities

- The system also provides for accountability. It ensures a higher level of responsibility and ownership of the overall activities in the assigned accounts

- The representatives would be required to makc courtesy calls in the slow periods. In order to make the customer feel that he/she is taken care of.

In model "b," the customer feels that he/she has to deal with one person, always knowing who to speak to. Solution "a" does not offer the kind of personalized service that the second offers. Model "b" would be reserved for a sales setting and model "a" for a big call center where people call occasionally, instead of periodically.

The Keys to the Success of a Customer Service Department:

- Proper policies, procedures and systems in place (a customer service philosophy should be instilled throughout the company)
- Adequate recruiting and training (behavioral and products/services)
- Overall knowledge of product and services with continuing education about products and services
- Clear understanding of customers' needs
- Professionalism in dealing with the customer
- Efficient resources and equipment
- Proper channeling of communication between the departments interacting with customer service.

The Skills Required for a Customer Service Representative

- Experience in customer service
- Good communicator, who is articulate with a good telephone voice
- Energetic, positive, good natured
- Enjoys working with and helping people
- Good presentation, interacts well with people
- Computer literate
- Willing to go the extra mile to satisfy the customer
- Patient in dealing with people.

Job Description

- Answer the phone
- Receive client calls
- Process customer requests
- Investigate and follow-up on client complaints
- Produce report of client complaints and copy all concerned parties/departments
- Remain current on products and services offered
- Make courtesy calls to the customers
- Keep a log of telephone calls received
- Keep a log of telephone calls issued, document the conversation and make an appointment on agenda of next date to call customer
- Communicate customer service issues to the other departments
- Maintain customer files and update contact name, address and telephone numbers
- Maintain and update customer service procedure manual
- Report account inactivity of major accounts to the customer service supervisor.

Department Structure

- Hours of operation
- Communication equipment needed:
  - Telephones with headset
  - Faxes and computers
- Customer Service Forms
- Customer lists
- Training manuals
- Procedure manuals
- Workstations
- Office supplies.

Recruitment Process

- Advertising for employees
- Job Description
- Interview process
- Develop training material and timeline
- Questionnaire of real-life customer service situations to be completed by the applicant
- Role-playing of customer interaction situations.

Training Process

- The company vision and mission
- What is our product/service?
- Advanced knowledge and continuing education on products and services offered
- Telephone etiquette
- How to deal with difficult or angry customers
- General communication skills
- Knowing our customers' needs
- Scenario development and role playing of real-life customer service situations
- Compliance
- Department forms, their applications and how to complete them.

Quality Improvement Initiatives

The customer service department should have meetings on an as-needed basis. These meetings will provide the employees with the opportunity to share their experience and discuss customer service issues. A segment of the meeting should be dedicated to the continuous training program for employees to learn about the existing and upcoming products and/or services.

Inspirational Quote

"We listened to what our customers wanted and acted on what they said. Good things happen when you pay attention".
- John F. Smith

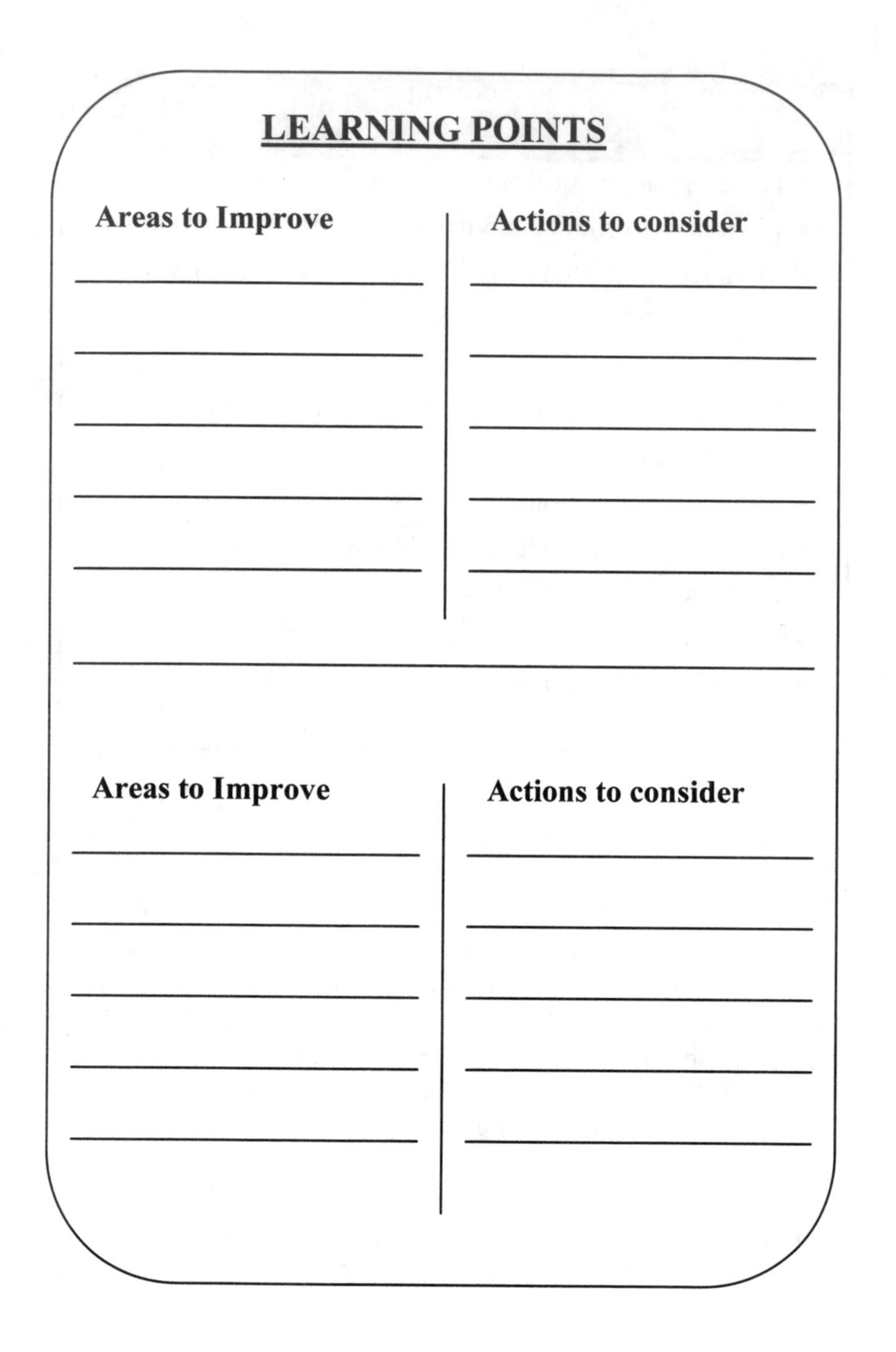
LEARNING POINTS
Areas to Improve
Actions to consider
Areas to Improve
Actions to consider

What I learned from this chapter:

NOTES

CHAPTER 6

ETHICS

Ethics is defined as the moral philosophy that directs the concepts of right and wrong. Ethics in this chapter will be for "Etiquette" because it addresses telephone and office etiquette and the dress code.

- Telephone and office etiquette
- Email etiquette
- The dress code
- How to deal with pushy people.

Telephone and Office Etiquette

The phone is sometimes the first and only contact a customer has with a company. As such, it becomes extremely important to answer the phone properly. You won't have a second opportunity to make a great impression on your customers. To ensure that the telephone is answered properly, enclosed are a few guidelines:

- Answer by the third ring
- Start with a greeting such as "Good Morning"
- Identify yourself or your company
- End with "How may I help you?"

I called American Express recently and the person at the other end answered: "How can I exceed your expectations today?" What a great way to answer the phone!

The person at the other end will not capture more than that. Sometimes people try to give too much information as they answer the phone. A company may try to include a sales pitch in the greeting. It's not a good idea. Instead, it is recommended that the personnel be trained to offer the special at the *end of the conversation.*

If you are asking the person at the other end to hold, give them notice of what you are doing. Obtain their approval first before placing them on hold. Give as much information as possible to the client on hold. Return to the phone often to explain what you are doing.

When taking a message, ask the caller their name, the name of company, telephone number and message if any. Remember to repeat the telephone number and ask for an alternate number and a window of time to call them back.

When answering the phone, enclosed are some suggestions of how to address the caller.

Do not use: Who is calling?
Use: May I ask who is calling?

Do not use: He or she is not in yet
Use: He or she is not available at the moment

Do not use: He is on vacation
Use: He is out of the office and will return on "give date of return"

Do not use: He is on a break
Use: He is away from his desk at the moment

Do not use: She is out sick today
Use: She is not in today

Do not use: He is busy now
Use: He is not available
Do not use: I have a customer, could you call back?

Use:	I have to finish something, can I call you back in X amount of time?

Do not use:	I have a customer, could you call back?
Use:	I have to finish something, can I call you back in X amount of time? Never ask customers to call back. It's your job to address their needs or take a message and return their calls

Do not use:	We are closed, can you call back tomorrow?
Use:	Most departments are closed at the moment. I will do my best to help you. However, I may have to finalize things tomorrow.

Refrain from providing any information concerning the whereabouts of an employee or co-worker. It does not look professional and gives a bad impression to the caller.

Email Etiquette

Email is replacing phone calls, chatting and the regular "Memorandum" in the office. It is such a great tool for communication. Today, many feel that email use is excessive. However, it is an excellent tool to communicate both with co-workers, your boss, suppliers and your customers.

Using email to communicate with co-workers is great but it must be used adequately. If an email is sent with an arrogant tone, it can be damaging to the sender. It is also important not to send any sexually suggestive email jokes or pictures on company email systems. That can become a source of disturbance and a cause for reprimand and/or dismissal. They can also bring sexual harassment lawsuits.

If an email is sent as a formal communication, it should be formatted like the original memorandum, with the proper addressing:

- Attention: name of recipient, title and department (title may not be necessary if internal)
- cc: carbon-copied individuals
- Don't use all caps when sending emails, it is considered "yelling" and is viewed as unfriendly
- Signature: you should have your signature at the end of the email including, your name, department, telephone, fax and email address. Don't include your company logo. Logos take a lot of space and will clog company email capacity. They are also difficult to upload. If your message is going to someone without high speed Internet, it will take a long time to upload. Having your information at the end of the email will enable people to refer to you

easily by having your information on-hand in the email.

BENEFITS OF EMAIL:	NEGATIVE IMPACT OF EMAIL:
• Communication is documented • Can be a task reminder • Can be kept on file for a long time on-line.	• Communication can become never-ending • It can be used for legal purposes against you or your company • Can be damaging if used to project anger.

When sending email, always remember to:

- ***Double check for spelling***
- ***Tone of message***
- ***Confirm that attachments and/or pictures are inserted, etc.***

The Dress Code

The workplace is a professional place. Unless your manager determines that the dress code is business-casual, the dress code is formal. It does not mean that one should wear a suit every day. It means that one should dress with clothes that express the business environment. The way you dress speaks loudly about who you are and what you represent. Your clothes are your uniform. If you have a police uniform, you are perceived as a police officer. Therefore, look professional if you want to portray a professional image.

Some companies require the ladies to wear hosiery. Others are more flexible. Most companies allow their employees to dress down on Fridays. This does not mean in anyway that it is acceptable to come in workout clothes, sweat pants, or revealing clothes. Using judgment will avoid any contradictions with management on this very sensitive subject. It is recommended that one adapts to the workplace dress code and also remain conservative to avoid any confusion.

How to Deal with Pushy People

Some believe that pushy people do not mean to be pushy. They are simply so focused and self-centered that they do not realize that they are annoying to others. Others feel that they are just work oriented and want to get things done right away. They feel that if they push and constantly annoy, they will get their way, and they usually do get their way. Why, because the not-so-pushy people give them what they want.

Having always gotten what they want right away, pushy people want to improve their performance by getting things faster. You have to be firm but fair. There are times when they really need what they are pushing for. However, since they sometimes cry wolf, it's difficult to determine when they have an emergency and when they are being frivolous. My recommendation is to ask honestly if they can wait or if they have a real crisis. If it's a real emergency, then help the person right away. If not, schedule a time to get things done.

Inspirational Quote
"Chance favors only the prepared mind".
Louis Pasteur

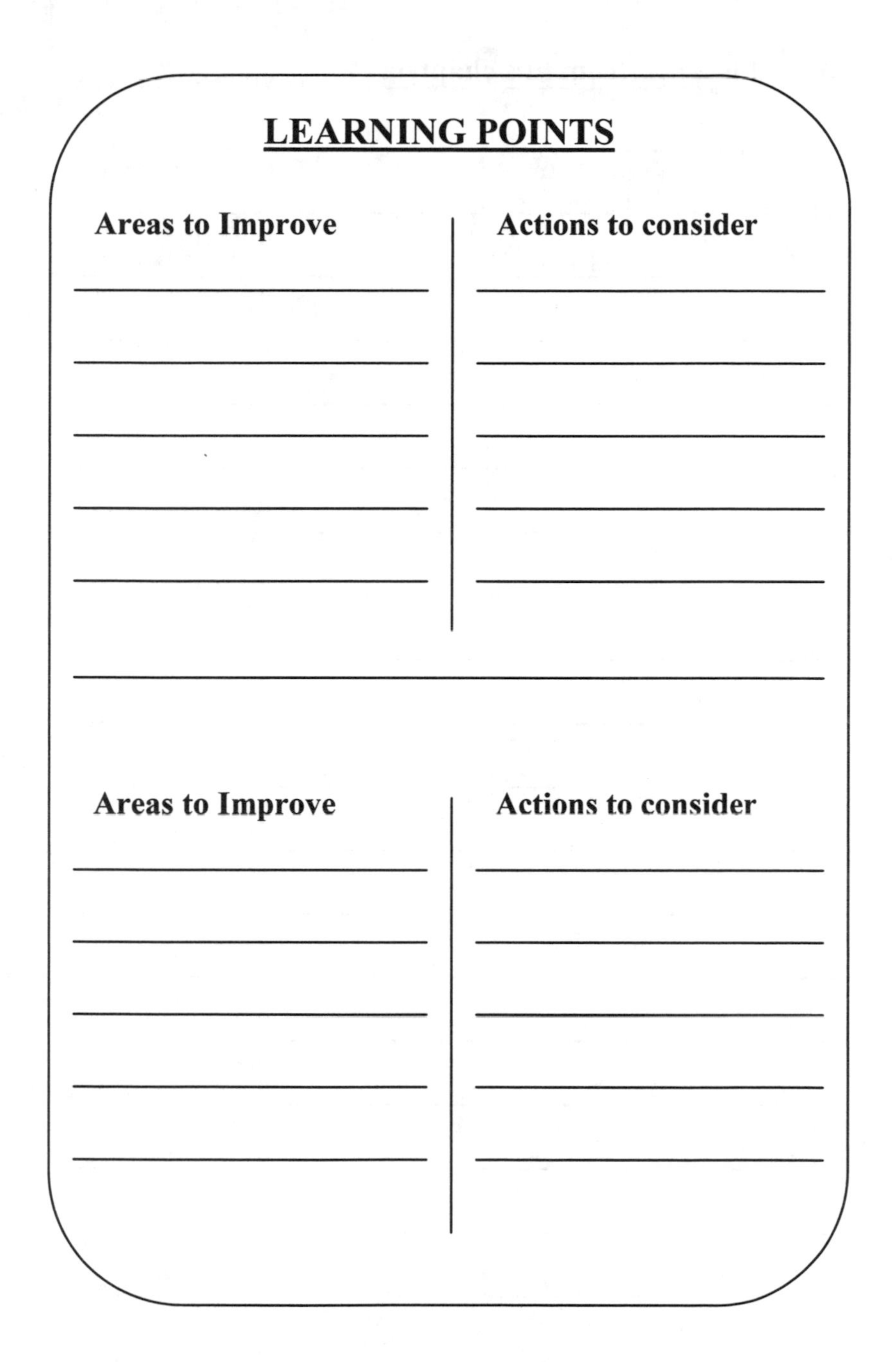
LEARNING POINTS
Areas to Improve
Actions to consider
Areas to Improve
Actions to consider

What I learned from this chapter:

NOTES

CHAPTER 7

TECHNOLOGY AND YOU

Technology has become the most important tool of this profession. A quick tour of Word and Outlook will be offered including some useful advanced commands.

Technological Advances

I have been in the workforce for a long time. I remember the manual typewriter! The upgraded IBM Selectric that cost a whopping $4000. I also remember the fax machine. What a great innovation that was! However, nothing has been more important in this position than the latest technologies. They are the main tools employed to produce your work. Technology has taken this job to a whole new level. Enclosed are some of the many programs used for this job. They are as follows:

- Word: to write letters, reports, flyers, etc.
- Excel: to compute numbers, create spreadsheets and make calculations, etc.
- PowerPoint: for presentations and reports
- Publisher: for publications, flyers, brochures, etc.
- Outlook: for email, calendar, contact management, appointments, reminders, tasks, etc.
- PDA: (Personal Digital Assistant) functions like a mobile outlook. There are many kinds. The Blackberry and the Palm function as a Cellular phone with email and contact management.
- Adobe: to create PDF files with enabled security and minimized hard drive space
- jpg: to work with images
- The list goes on. It almost feels like a new product or program is born every day.

Although the list of innovations is impressive, nothing has impacted our lives like the Internet. It has revolutionized the way we do business, communicate, work, play, gamble and date, etc. It is such an amazing tool. I can't imagine life without it. How did we ever live without it? We have everything at our fingertips: from researching companies to contract work, manufacturers, information, shopping, supplies, etc. The possibilities are endless. The information available is overwhelming. Never have we had such an amazing amount of information available in one place. Some of the greatest search engines are: Google, MSN, Yahoo, Dogpile, Ask, etc.

If you work as an Administrative Assistant and have yet to use the Internet for your work, you should really consider taking some classes. It is as important as Microsoft's Office Suite, including: Word, Excel and Outlook.

The reader of this book should have basic understanding of the computer and the Microsoft Office programs. In this chapter, some basic computer skills in Word and Outlook will be covered. They are among the most used programs in the office.

MS Word Basics

Toolbar: Shown on top of the screen. They are the variety of icons that are used to execute commands. The commands are found on the enclosed drop down menus:

1. File
2. Edit
3. Insert
4. Format
5. Tools
6. Table
7. Windows
8. Help

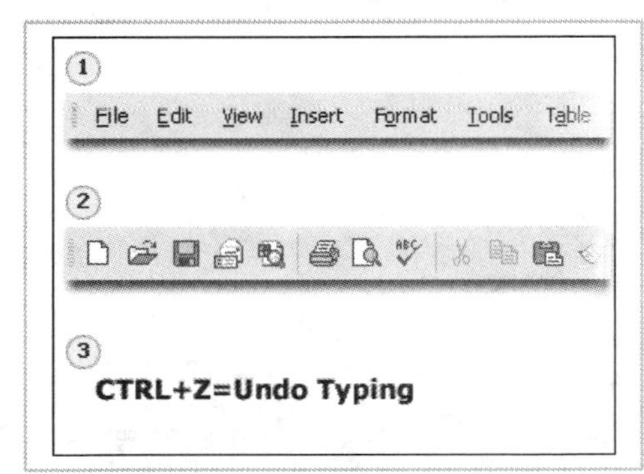

The technology section follows the natural flow of the drop down menus. The commands, and most of their uses, will be explored. Some of the most difficult commands will not be reviewed. They should be learned in a classroom. At the end of each program segment, a list of shortcuts for both Word and Outlook is provided.

Using Word

1. FILE

Creating of a new document or file

Click on the "File" menu. Click on "New" and choose between a blank document and a template.

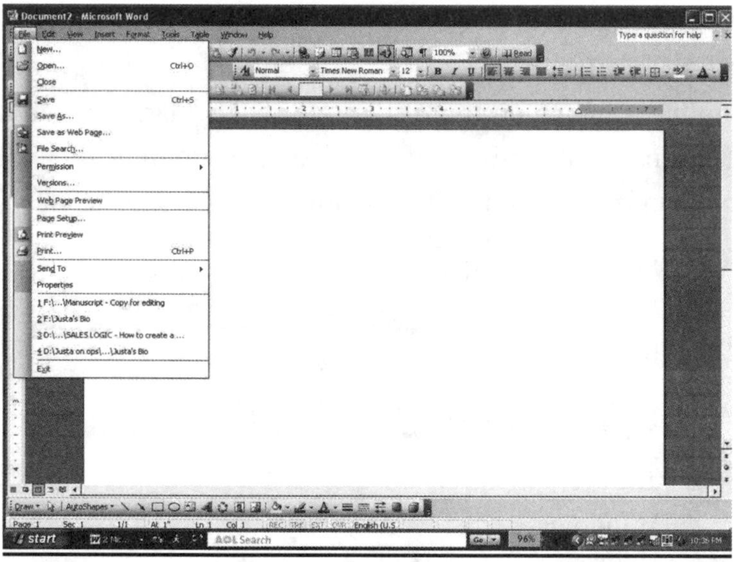

Opening an existing document

To open an existing document, you can access the document from "Explore." To open "Explore," go to the "Start" menu, right click on "Start" and click on "Explore." This will open the file folders. Once you find the desired file, double click on the file and it will open.

The second way to open an existing document is to go the "File" menu, click on "Open" and search for the desired document.

Formatting a page

To format a page or give the page a special size: click on the "File" menu. Go to "Page Set Up," use the "Margin" grid to pick the size of your document.

To pick the layout, while still in "File" go to "Paper Size" and pick the layout. If you want the document to be vertical pick "Portrait" and for horizontal pick "Landscape." Once you chose the format, the whole document will have the same size.

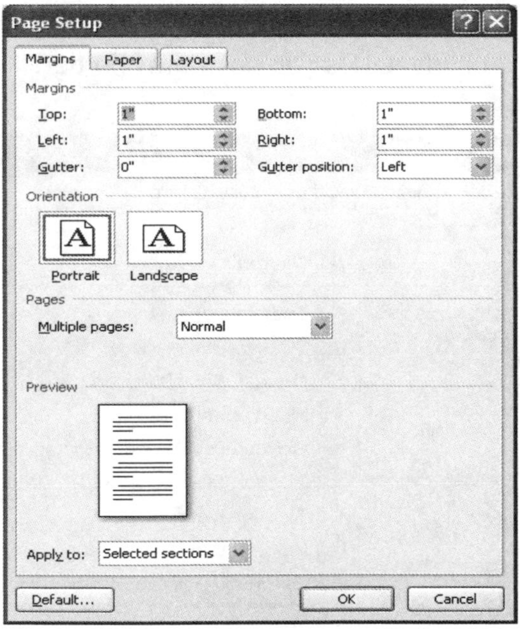

Filing a document into drawers called "Folders"

The computer saving capacity acts like a filing cabinet. You can put your files in different drawers called "Folders." You can organize your documents in these folders.

To create the "Folders" (or label the drawers,) right click on the "Start" button and click on "Explore." Once open, pick the filing cabinet or location where you wish to open the new folder. You can use "My Documents" to file on your computer or an outside CD, floppy or flash drive. Once on the location, click i.e. "My Documents," then click on the file menu and name the new file.

Be specific with the names you give your folder because your file will be inside the "Folder," and you won't have access to your file unless you open the "Folder."

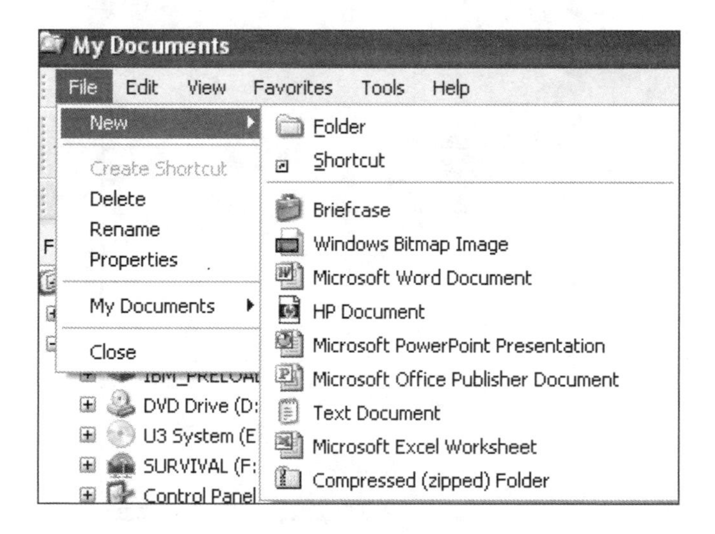

Printing functions

Click on the "File" menu, click on "Print." If you need specific printing options, use that mode. If you want to print the whole document, you can simply click on the printer icon on the toolbar. Using shortcut "Ctrl-P" will bring the printing command menu. You can print one page, multiple pages or the whole document.

To print one page, hit CTRL-P, pick "Current Page" from the "Page Range" or insert the page number in the window called "Page." To print a section, CTRL-P, insert the pages i.e. 1-3 in the "Page" section. You can also print multiple copies by clicking the up and down arrows in the "Number of Copies" field and pick the number of copies desired.

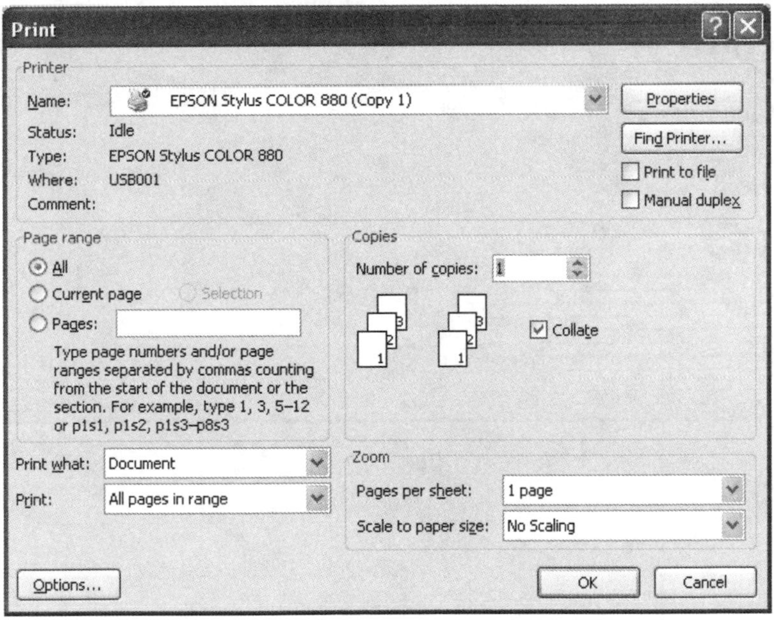

Saving functions

It is recommended that you save a document at the creation and to save continuously as you type. This will prevent losing your work should you lose power or the computer shuts down accidentally. You can also use "AutoSave," shown further.

To save a document, Click on the "File" menu, click on "Save As." This command will be used the first time you need to save a document. The first step is to "Name" the document or file. Use a name that will be easy to remember for future retrievals.

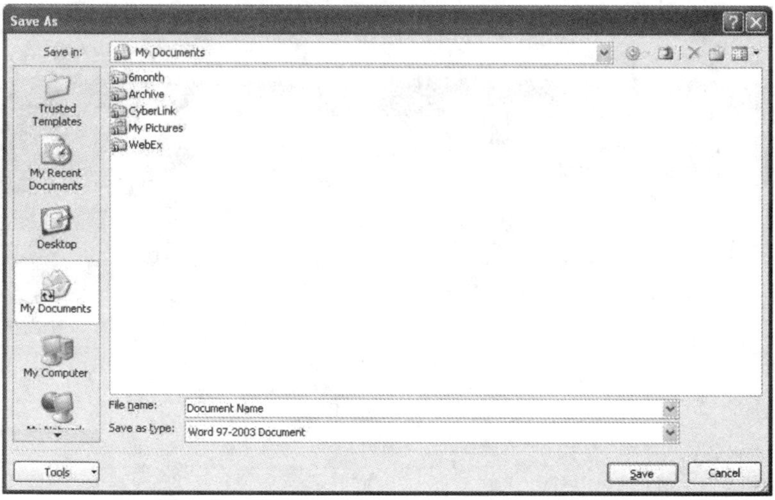

Setting Auto-Save - will prevent losing a document in case of power failure or accidental shut down of computer.

- From the "Tools" menu, go to "Options,"
- Go to the "Save" tab
- Next to the "Minutes Counter," click the button for "Save AutoRecover info every" and choose the number of minutes, 5 or 10 minutes is suggested.

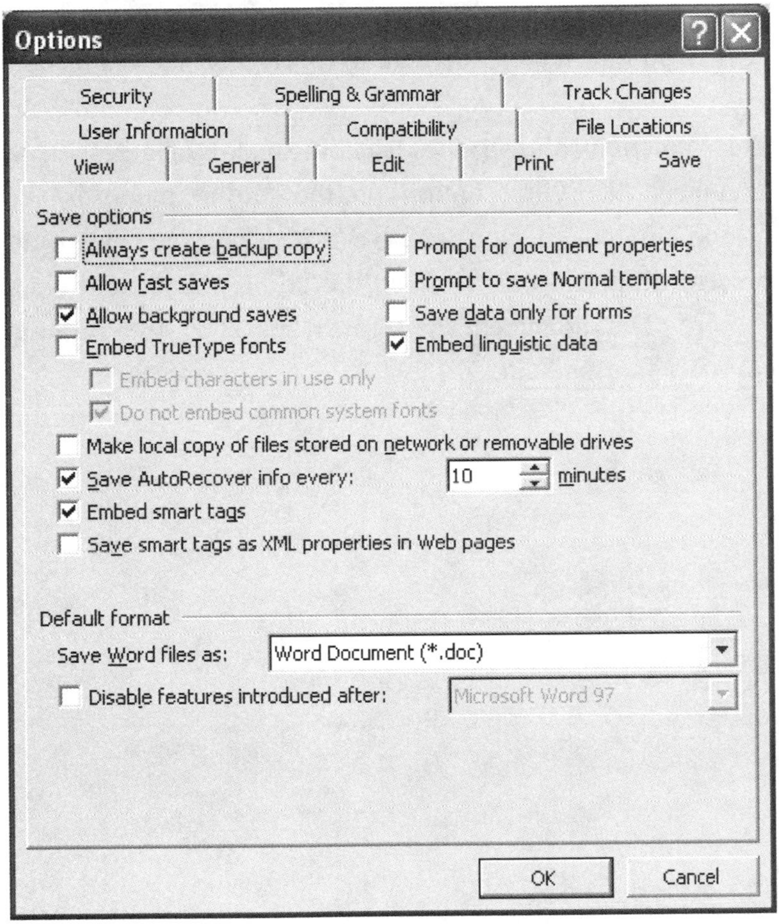

2. EDIT

Editing capacities

Word has the capacity to return a document to its original state by using the "Undo" button. One example is if you typed or formatted a document in error. You can also use "Undo" to return the document to its original state.

This function allows the user to make changes in a document. The first option on the "Edit" menu is the "Undo" menu. If you remove something and want to reverse what you did, click on the "Edit" menu, and click "Undo" The document will revert back to the original format. (Shortcut: Ctrl-Z.)

Replacing an unwanted word: “Find and Replace”

To search for a specific word, from the “Edit” function on the Toolbar, and click “Find” (Shortcut: Ctrl-F.) You can either change or replace the word. You can use this function to replace the same word with a new word. You can also change the same word typed multiple times by using this function on the Replace tab and clicking “Replace All.”

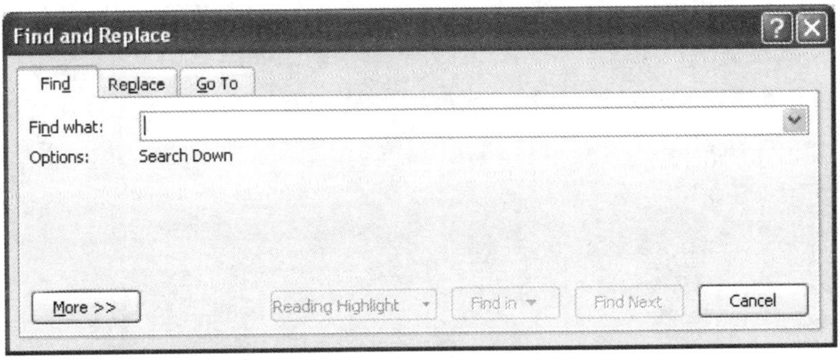

Copy and paste

This function allows the user to copy a word, sentence, paragraph or whole document. To copy, highlight the area to be copied, click "Edit" then click on "Copy" (Shortcut: CTRL-C) and go to the desired place where the area is to be copied. Click on "Paste" (Shortcut: CTRL-V) to paste the copied item. To Select the whole document, from the "Edit" menu on the Toolbar, click "Select All" or use the Shortcut: CTRL-A.

3. VIEW

Different ways to view a document

To review your document, click on the "View" menu which will allow you to view the page you are working on in various layouts: "Normal," "Web," "Print" or "Outline" layout.

This function will also give you the "Toolbar" options. The toolbar is the tool that allows you to control everything from "Font Size" to "Copy and paste," etc. It is simply the display on top of the screen.

Essentials from the toolbar display include: "Standard" and "Formatting," which are vital functions to edit your document.

Using the toolbar

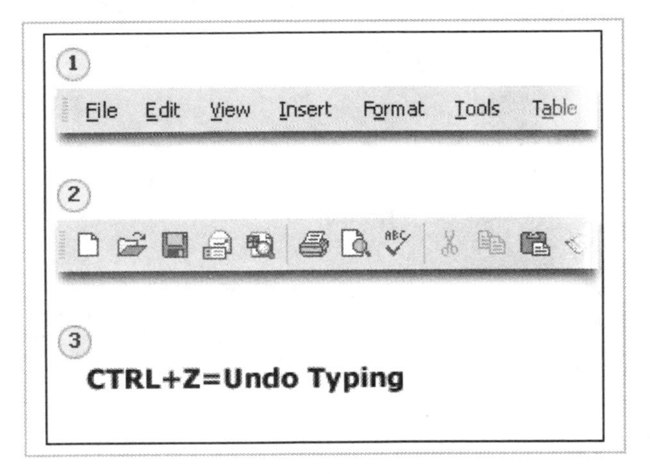

When you click on the "Toolbar" option, you can arrange the various icons that will allow you to work easier without using the pull down menus. The main and basic functions are “Standard,” “Formatting” and “Drawing.” Their uses are as follows:

Standard: when you choose “Standard”, you will have the icons as shown on line two (2) of the “Toolbar Picture.” These icons will allow you to: “Open” a document, “Print,” “View,” “Copy and Paste,” “Undo,” and “Size” the screen, etc.

Formatting: allows you to pick your “Font” “Type,” “Size,” “Bold,” “Italic,” “Underline,” “Align,” “Bullets,” “Borders,” “Color” and “Font Color.”

Drawing: will show at the bottom of your screen and allow you to “Draw Shapes” and “Autoshapes”, “Insert Pictures,” “Color” the borders of the squares, “Font Size” and “Color,“ etc.

Using header and footer

This is a great tool to create a document that has a uniform title (header) and page number or other information (footer) placed at the bottom at the page.

Using the "Header and Footer" commands, you can insert typing, title, company logo, pictures, page numbers, date, time, name of file owner, etc. It's a neat way to have each page identically titled, dated, etc.

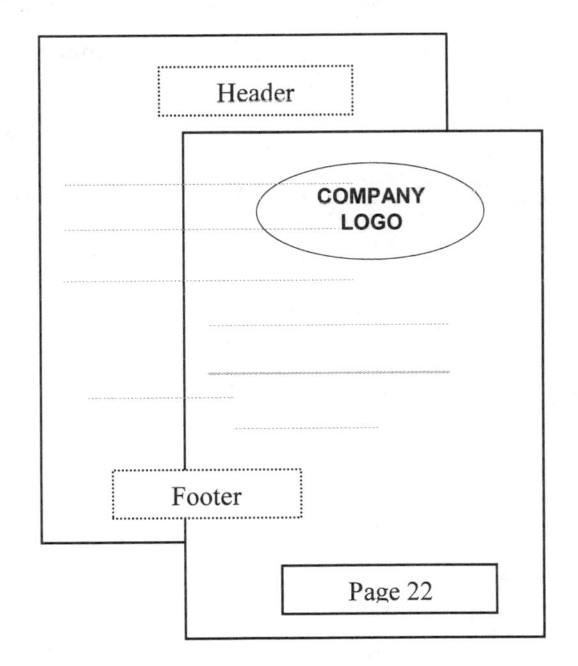

4. INSERT

Inserting a page

Easiest way to insert a page is to press: "CTRL Enter."

Inserting page number

Page numbering is easier in the: "Header-Footer" function found in the "View" drop down menu "Insert AutoText." This will let you insert a special page number or page number format: "Page X of Y."

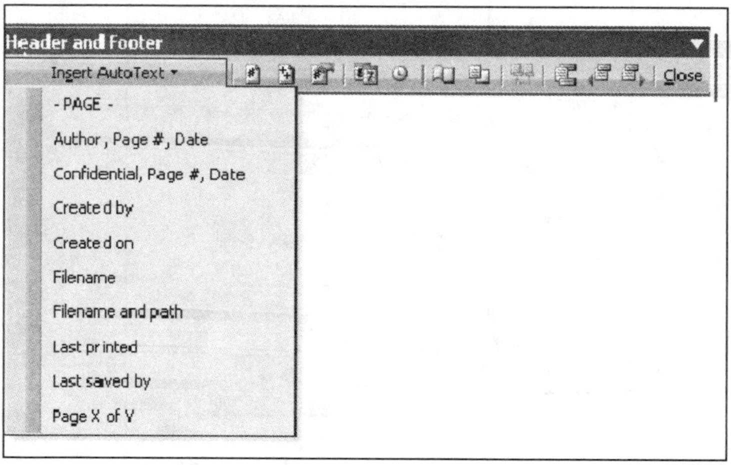

Inserting symbols

International alphabets and symbols such as: é, ñ, etc., are found in the “Insert” drop down menu. Click “Symbol” to look for the symbol or letter. Insert desired “Symbol.”

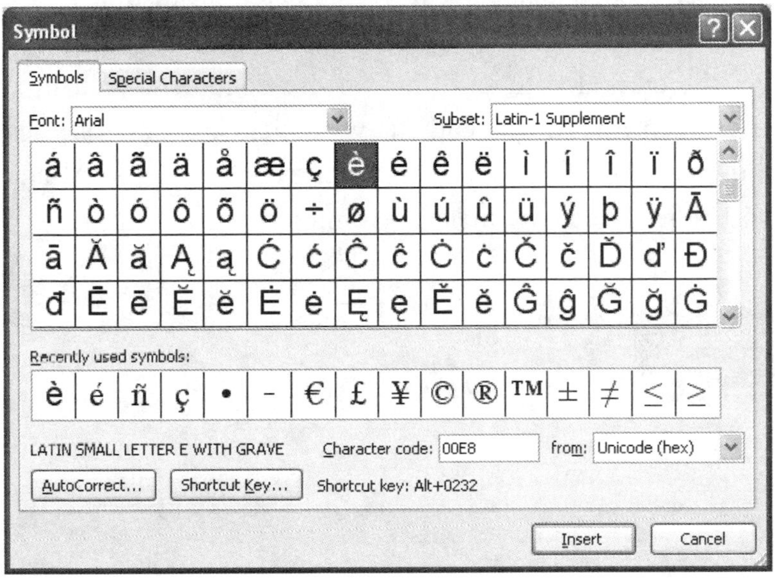

Inserting date and time

Go to "Insert" and select "Date and Time." Choose the format you wish to appear on the document.

To keep a document current with updated "Date and Time" every time, just click on "Update Automatically." This will put the current date and time on the document each time you open the document. If you pick this option, the previous or original date of the document will not show and will be replaced with the current information.

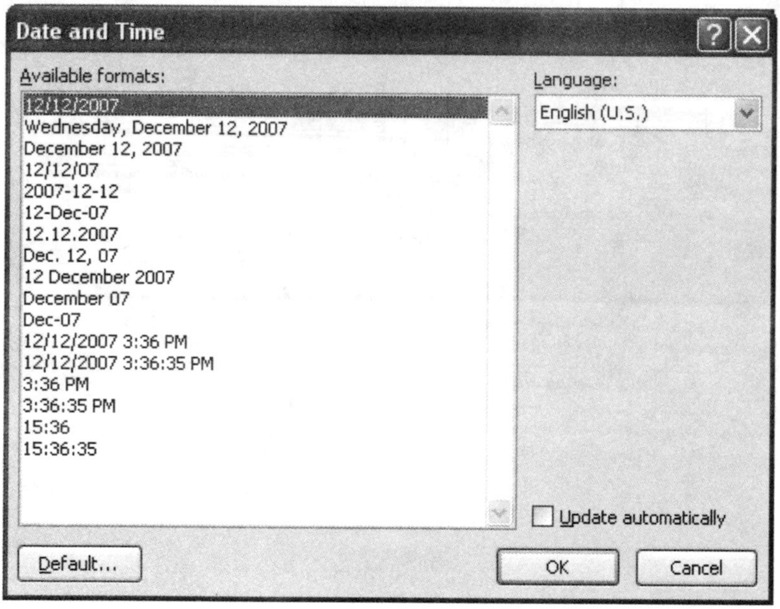

Date and Time

Available formats:

12/12/2007
Wednesday, December 12, 2007
December 12, 2007
12/12/07
2007-12-12
12-Dec-07
12.12.2007
Dec. 12, 07
12 December 2007
December 07
Dec-07
12/12/2007 3:36 PM
12/12/2007 3:36:35 PM
3:36 PM
3:36:35 PM
15:36
15:36:35

Language:

English (U.S.)

Update automatically

Default...

OK

Cancel

Insert autotext: Attn, Salutations, Page X of Y…

This function serves to insert predetermined "Attention Lines," "Closing Lines," "Salutations," for example, "Closing" at the end of a letter such as: "Yours truly," etc.

To use this command, click on "Insert," choose "AutoText" and pick a line.

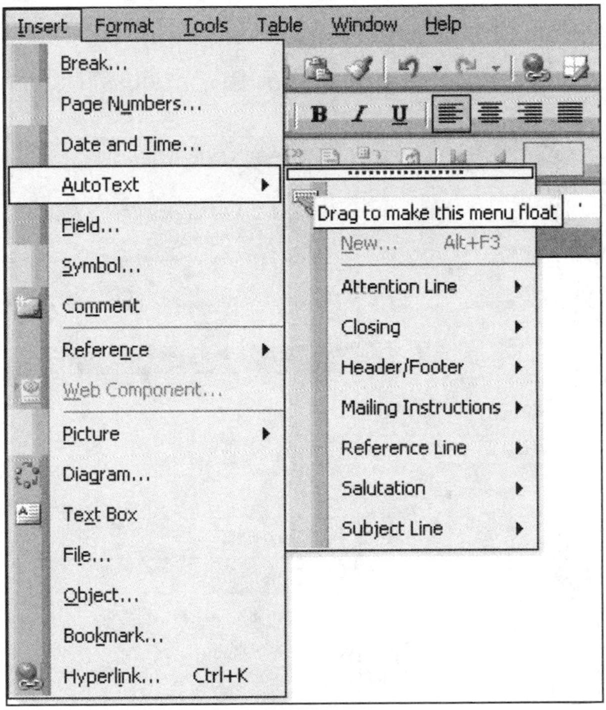

Insert pictures and files

Go to "Insert," click on "Picture" and choose either a picture from a file or "Clip Art." To manage the picture better, prior to inserting the picture, create a "Drawing Box." The box is shown at the bottom of the "Drawing" screen. Click on the box to bring it on the screen. Right click on the box to "Add Text." You can then insert the picture directly into the box. The box makes it easier to move the picture around the screen. You don't need a box to insert a "Picture". It just makes the process easier.

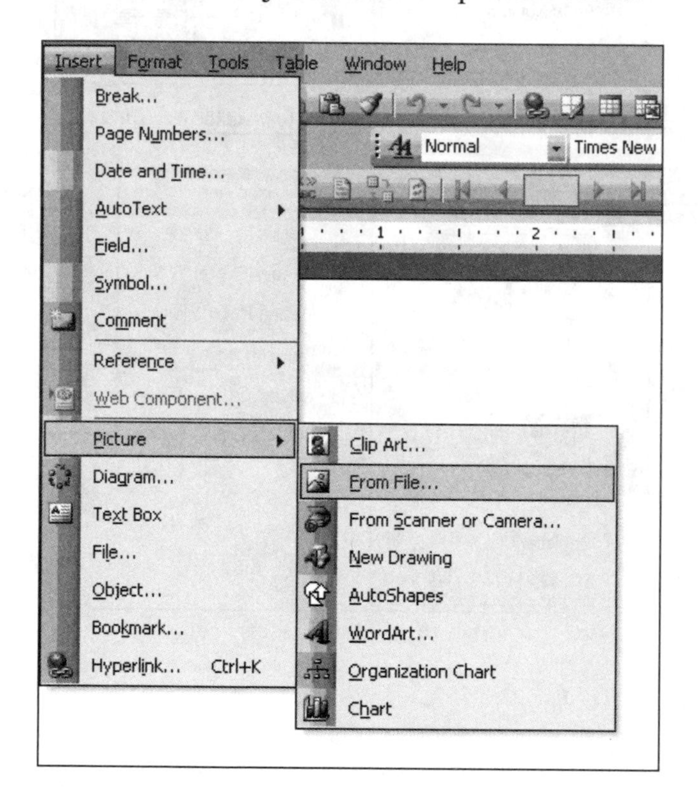

5. FORMAT

Fonts (lettering type)

You can select various types of letters referred to as "Fonts" in Word and all other Microsoft Office programs.

The fonts are the first option on the "Format" drop down menu. You can view the fonts and what they look like from that option then select the font you want.

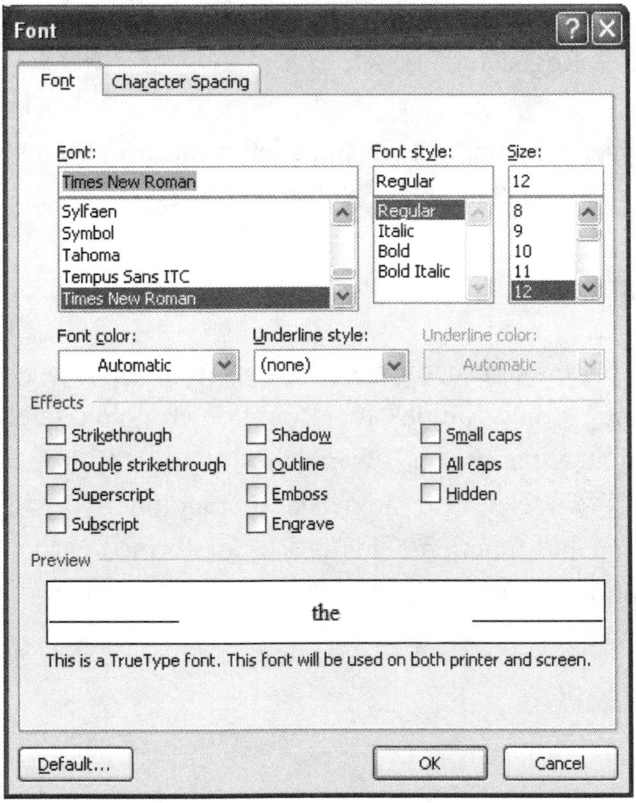

Small caps

You can make your letters small caps (SMALL CAPS) or all caps (ALL CAPS.) You can pick these options from the "Font" screen.

Superscript (x^2) or Subscript (x_2)

To make the letter "Superscript," highlight the symbol and choose the option "Superscript" in the "Font" window. This makes your letters rise next to a word such as Trade Mark™, Registered® or X^2.

To achieve the opposite or put a letter under or "Subscript," follow the same and pick "Subscript" X_2.

Paragraph

Most common use of paragraph is to format the "Line Spacing" from "Single" to "Double," etc. You select and highlight: "Paragraph" from the "Format" drop down menu. You can also align the paragraph by using the "Alignment" function. This task is performed easier using the buttons from the "Toolbar" on top of the screen.

Bullet and numbering

To insert bullets or numbered line items, you can go to "Format," click on "Bullets and Numbering." You can choose the required format. At times, the bullets or the numbers may create a problem with alignment, to correct that problem, use the ruler on the top to align the lines. You can choose from multiple types of bullet and number formats.

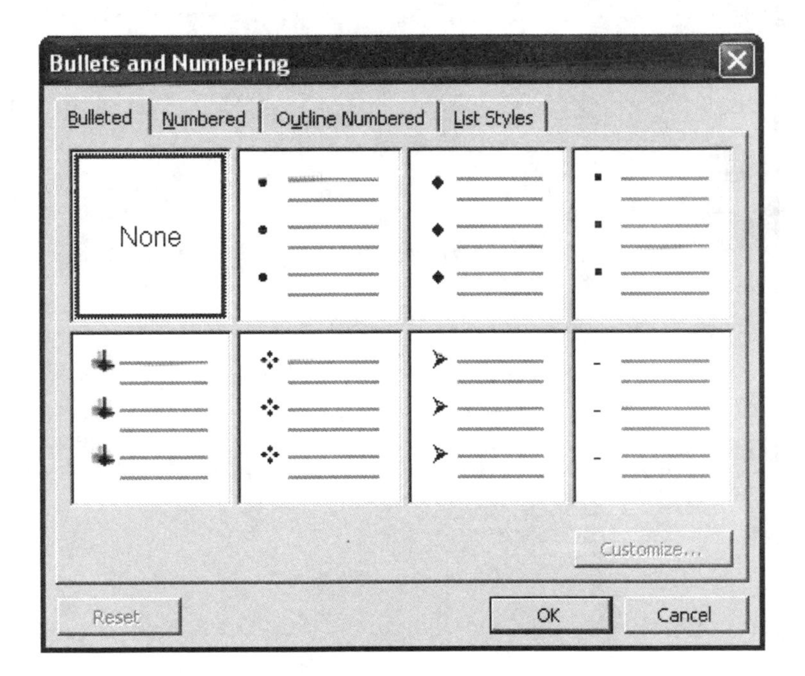

Border and shading

You must first create a table from the "Table" function in order to enable this function easier. The first "Tab" is the border function, which will format the table borders. The second tab is to format the "Page Border" and the last tab is to color the table or put "Shade" on the table.

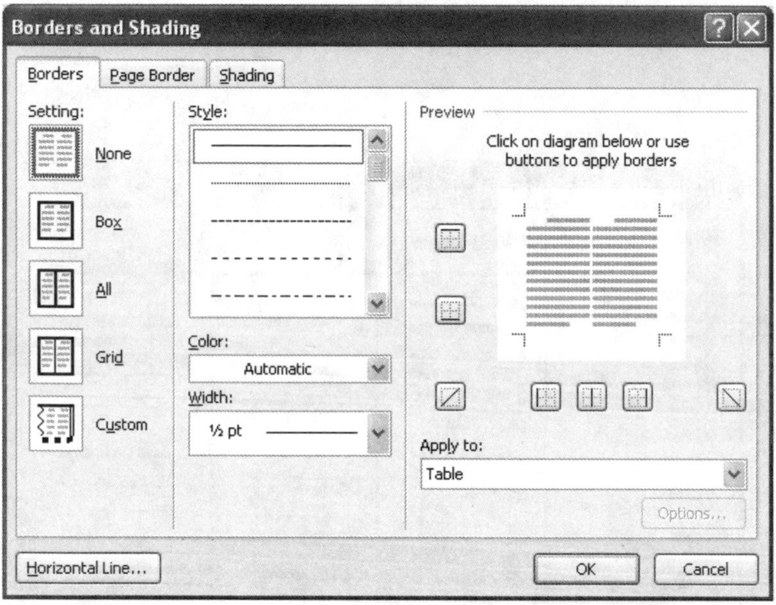

Change case - used to change the size of your font

If you typed in small letters and want to change to either capital letters or sentence style, you can highlight the desired words and in the format drop down menu, pick "Change Case" to change your font size.

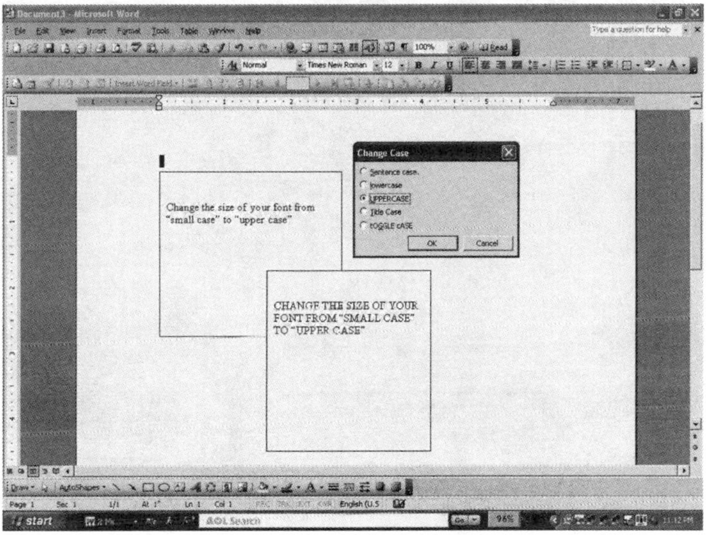

Columns

You can use the “Column” function from the “Format” drop down menu or use the “Table” function by going to “Table” and inserting one.

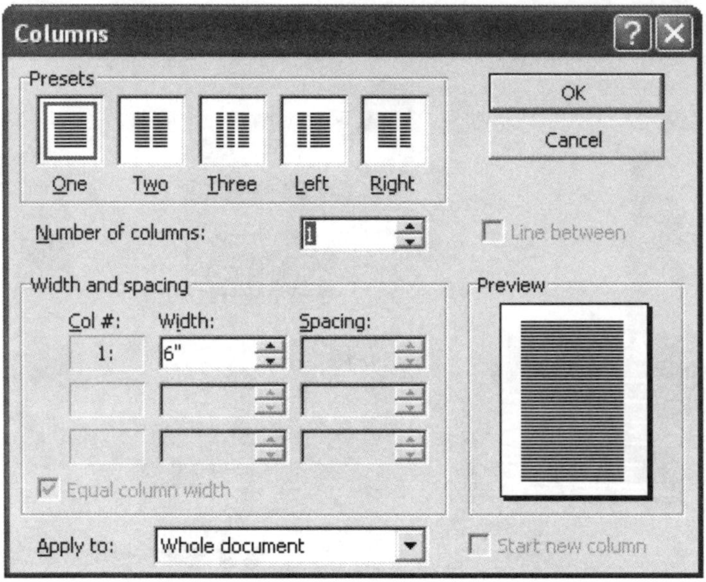

Text direction

To achieve this, a table or column is required. First, pick either from the "Column" or "Table" format.

From the "Format" drop down menu, pick the "Text Direction" function and apply the direction required. This is a very fancy look for a more advanced document.

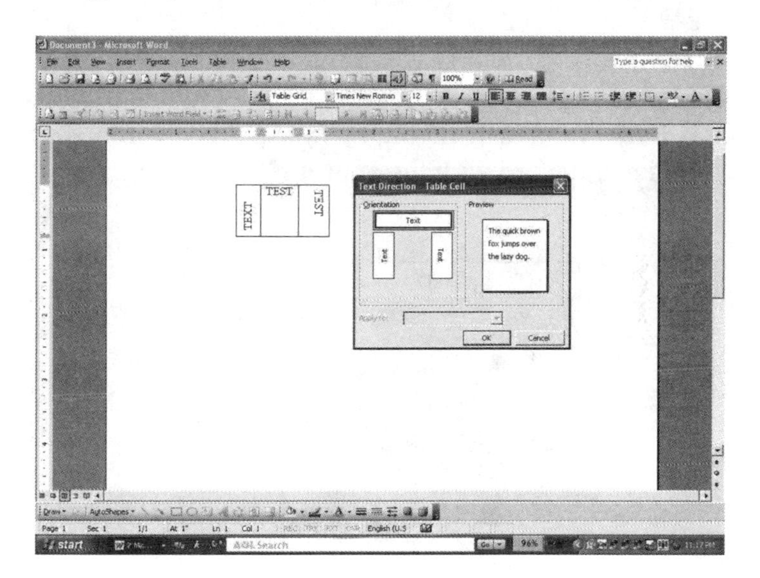

6. TOOLS

Spelling and grammar

This function is used to ensure that all your words are spelled correctly. If the word is misspelled by a word with different meaning, the wrong spelling many not be detected. This is a reviewing function.

To start the "Spell Check," go to: "Tools" from the drop down menu, pick "Spelling and Grammar" (Shortcut: CTRL F7.) Word will highlight misspelled words so you can replace the word with the appropriate spelling.

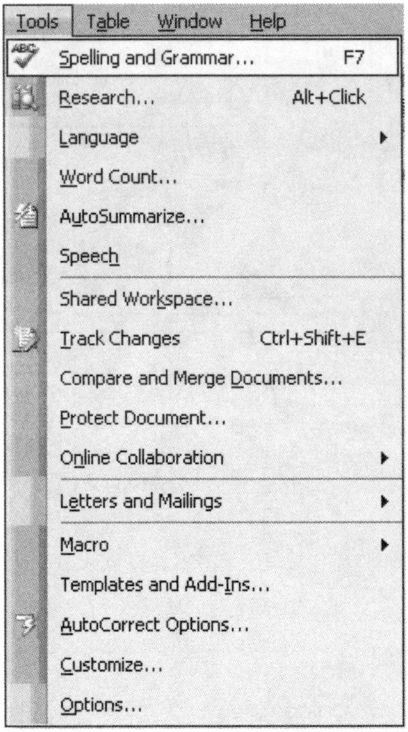

Tools Table Window Help
Spelling and Grammar... F7
Research... Alt+Click
Language
Word Count...
AutoSummarize...
Speech
Shared Workspace...
Track Changes Ctrl+Shift+E
Compare and Merge Documents...
Protect Document...
Online Collaboration
Letters and Mailings
Macro
Templates and Add-Ins...
AutoCorrect Options...
Customize...
Options...

Thesaurus

Another great time saving feature is the “Thesaurus.” It contains the use of a Thesaurus and dictionary instead of referring to a real book. The “Thesaurus” finds alternate or synonymous words to replace or substitute a word.

Addressing and creating envelopes

You can customize envelopes to specific sizes. This function is great for creating a few envelopes. Go to “Tools.” Then, click on “Letters and Mailing.” Pick: “Envelopes and Labels.” You can insert the address of the recipient. You can save your name and address as the sender. Just click on “Yes” when asked if you wish to save your name at the end of the process.

To create multiple envelopes, it is preferable to create labels and affix them to the envelopes. This is a function of “Mail Merge” found in “Tools” and reviewed in the “Mail Merge” section.

Language

To select which language you want your Word grammar to be activated with, go to the "Language" from the drop down menu and select your language.

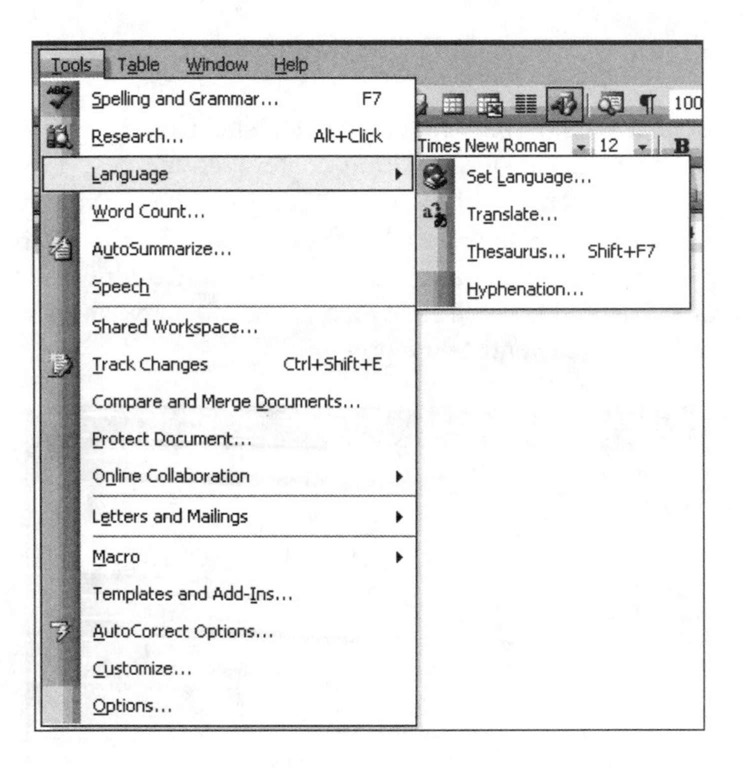

Word Count: counting the number of words typed

If you are doing work that requires counting the number of words typed, you can use this function. Go to the "Word Count" from the drop down menu and the information will be displayed.

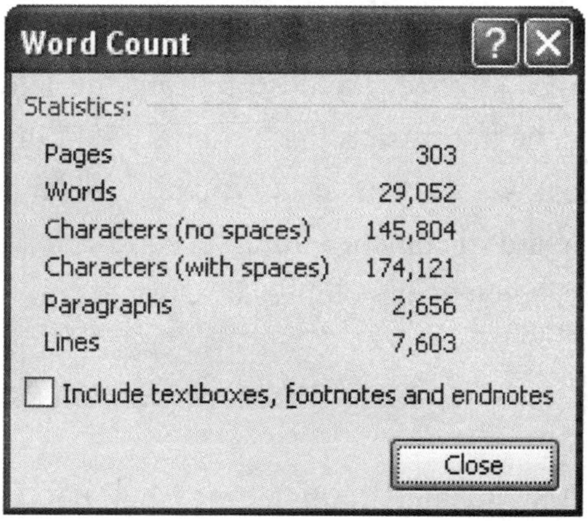

Word Count

Statistics:

Pages	303
Words	29,052
Characters (no spaces)	145,804
Characters (with spaces)	174,121
Paragraphs	2,656
Lines	7,603

Include textboxes, footnotes and endnotes

Close

Merge letters and labels

Merging is the feature that saves the most time in Word. Imagine creating one letter, post card or label and being able to customize this one document to send it to one to five hundred people. The reason why there is a limitation to five hundred is the amount of space required to store five hundred documents and for a typical printer to print five hundred pages at once. By customizing the letter, it gives your clients the impression that you only sent this one letter made especially for them. It is typically a combined effort between a word document and a spreadsheet. This is great to personalize letters, envelopes, labels, etc.

Mail merge uses three (3) different elements

1. The main document: the letter, label, post card or any other document you create for the merge
2. The data file or data source. This is easier if stored as a spreadsheet. Therefore, your data source is your SPREADSHEET. This is the list that contains your first name, last name, address, city, state/province and zip or postal code. It will be used to merge the letter to the names
3. The template created to include the address block to enable the mail merge.

The steps to create a mail merge

Step 1 - Prepare the spreadsheet to insert the data for names and addresses to be merged

First, create a spreadsheet with the columns showing:

- Names (separate first name and last name). This gives you the flexibility to greet customers by their first names
- Address
- City
- State
- Zip code.

Remember to create the headers, i.e. "Name," "Address," "City," "State" and "Zip Code" in separate columns starting from cell "A1." No column should be left empty vertically or horizontally.

In each row, include the information for each person to be included in the merge. Each row represents a complete record for a client. It contains the name, address, city, state and zip code of the client.

It's these columns and rows that make it possible to get unique information to a document during a mail merge.

P.S. Once the data is completely entered in the spreadsheet, it is very important to delimit the printing area by activating

"Set Printing Area" in Excel. This includes the whole area containing names and addresses to be used in the merge.

Create the spreadsheet as indicated in the illustration.

	A	B	C
1	**Name**	**Last Name**	**Street Address**
2	Nancy	Anderson	123 Main St.
3	Ann	Beebe	567 Country Rd.
4			
5			
6			
7			
8			
9			

Step 2 - Create the document to be merged

You can create the document ahead of time. For instance to create a letter, write the letter as usual. When the letter is finished it must be perfect because once merged, changes are difficult to make (except for changing words with "Find" and "Replace".)

Bring the letter to be merged to the window:

```
---------------

---------------

Dear ------,

------------------------------------------------------------
------------------------------------------------------------
------------------------------------------------------------

------------------------------------------------------------
------------------------------------------------------------
------------------------------------------------------------

--------------------
--------------------
```

Go to the "Mail Merge" section of the drop down menu.

Pick (1): Main Document; Click on "Create." Choose between, "Form Letters," "Mailing Labels," "Envelopes" or "Catalog." Pick "Form Letter" from "Active Window."

Go to (2) "Open Data Source." That is where it becomes difficult and if the spreadsheet is not done as described earlier, this will fail. Pick "Open Data Source" (your spreadsheet is your data source.) Remember to choose the file as an .xls or Excel type file (since the spreadsheet is your "Data Source".) Pick the "Print Area" and not the "Entire Spreadsheet." Once you select the "Print Area," the "Mail Merge Helper" will prompt you to "Edit Main Document."

What you are doing in this step is to mirror the categories on the spreadsheet to the main document so that when you merge, the spreadsheet can recognize where to insert each field in the right category.

Step 3 – Finalize the merge

Editing the main document: to insert the "Merge Field" or reporting the headers from the spreadsheet to your letter. This will enable the names, addresses, and other headers to become catalysts for the merge to happen. Headers will be inserted from "Insert Merge Field" commands that appear at the left corner of the top of the screen.

Click on the "Insert Merge Field" and insert the name, address, city, state, etc. to the document. Remember to place the field in the right order. Use the enclosed "Address Block" as your guide to ensure that the formatting of the letter is done properly.

What you will use from Excel to merge

"Address Block:"	« First Name» «Last Name» «Address» «City», «State» «Zip»

What the address will look like after the merge

"Address Block:"	John Smith 120 Hope Street, Apt 1 Hope, Utah 22222

Remember to use the recipient's first name next to "Dear." It's easier to merge with the first name, otherwise you will need to identify males from females in your spreadsheet or data source to insert Mr. and Mrs.

«Address Book»

Dear «First Name»,

Once this portion is completed, it's time to merge.

Go to "Mail Merge" and choose "Merge." This will merge your Word document to the names, address, etc. from the chosen spreadsheet.

The beauty of this command is that not only it saves you time but it also allows you to keep your name list on file in a different file on a spreadsheet. You can use the same name list or data source multiple times for different projects. You can create multiple documents and merge to the same group. Imagine how long it would take to type each letter with the name, address, etc!

Create an envelope from the "File" menu

An easier way to create an envelope is found in the "File" drop down menu. It is in the "Page Set-Up." This offers the ability to create an envelope from the second tab "Paper Size." Simply choose the size of the envelope and it will appear on your window. You can also customize the envelope size if not found in the choices. A template of the envelope can be saved with the sender's address for future use. The second way to create an envelope, Go to "Tools," you can create an envelope and you can also merge an envelope.

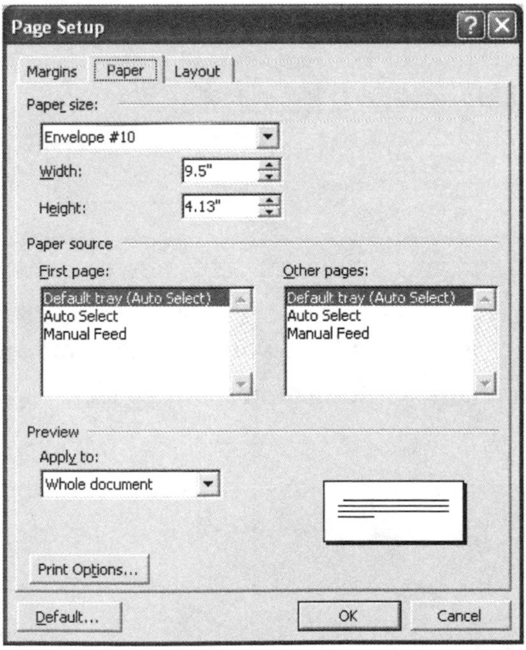

To create an envelope from the "Tools" menu

Go to "Tools:" click on "Envelope and Labels" Click on "Envelopes." Once in that window, you can write the name of sender and recipient. The name of recipient will be erased once the envelope is printed. However, when closing the dialog box, Word will request if you want to save the name of sender. If you reply yes, the next time you open the "Envelope" Dialog Box, the name of the sender will remain in the "Return Address" box.

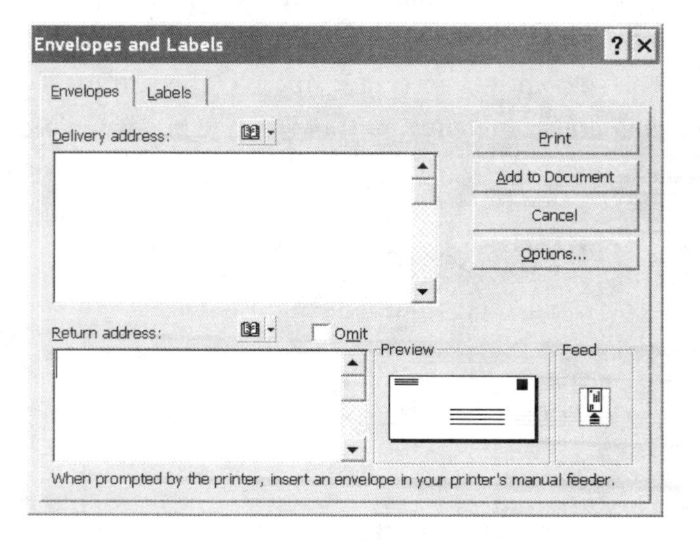

This feature is great to keep your private name and address or your company's information as the sender.

Labels

Creating labels: This function allows the user to create: business cards, CD labels, name cards, post cards, name tents and rotary cards, etc.

To create labels, go to the "Envelope and Labels" menu. Pick the "Labels" tab. Choose the label number (found on the label package.) If you don't have a label number, measure the label and try from the sizes that appear on the menu. Pick a number that matches the size you need and use that label number.

Once the number is chosen, click on "New Document" and a Word window will mimic the label on the screen. You can then type your information. To merge labels, follow the "Mail Merge" directions.

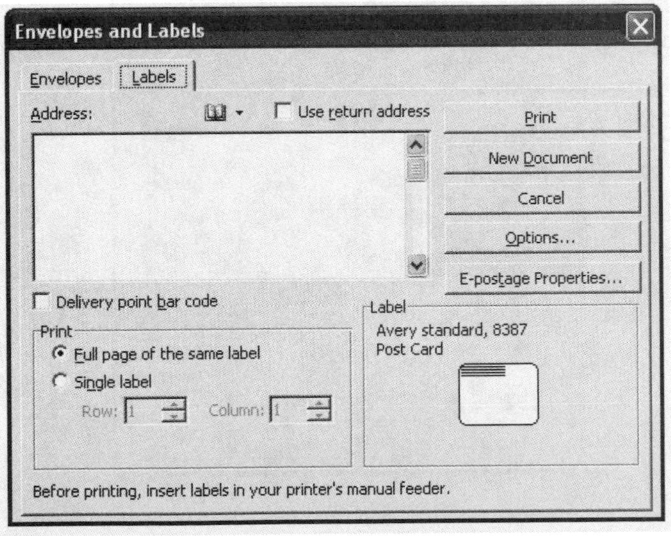

7. TABLE

A table in a document provides different opportunities to:

a) Organize information
b) Create visual interest
c) Work with columns that are easier to manage than the actual Word "Column" function found in the "Format" drop down menu.

Create a table

To create a table or columns, with special formatting colors and types, this is the command. From the "Table" menu, click on "Insert" and choose "Table."

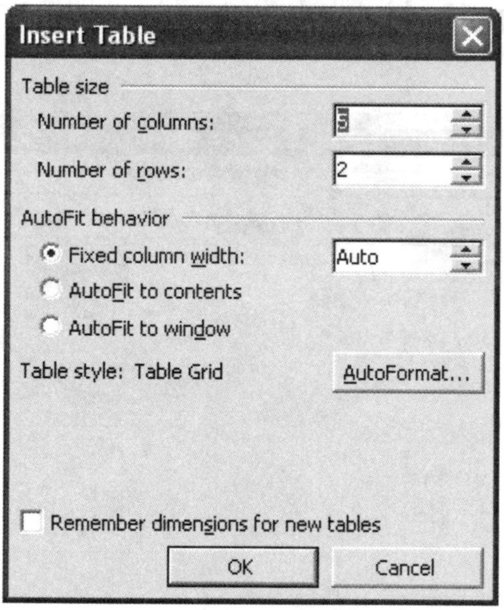

Insert Table
Table size
Number of columns: 3
Number of rows: 2
AutoFit behavior
Fixed column width: Auto
AutoFit to contents
AutoFit to window
Table style: Table Grid
AutoFormat...
Remember dimensions for new tables
OK
Cancel

Select the number of columns and rows you wish to have on the table. The enclosed table has 2 columns and 3 rows (not counting the shaded areas.)

Columns		
Rows		

To move within the columns and rows, press the "Tab" key to move from cell to cell or click the mouse in the desired cell. If you move with the tab to the last cell, the next time you move the tab, you will create an additional row. To cancel the row, click "Undo."

Resize a column, a cell or a row

To quickly resize a column, cell or a row in a table, refer to the "Table Properties" dialog box. This dialog box has tabs for formatting a table, a column, a row and a cell.

Distribute columns and rows evenly

Go to the "AutoFit" dialog box and choose between the multiple choices. To distribute columns and rows evenly, just click on that option while the columns and rows are highlighted.

Insert rows/columns

You can add columns and rows by using the "Insert" "Rows Above," "Rows Below," "Column To The Right," or "Column To The Left" from the "Table" drop down menu.

Merge cells

To create a table with different looks you can select a column of multiple rows and merge them into one cell.

This table is the original table

You can create tables with or without printing borders. To see the borders, just leave the table as is. To not see the table borders, on the "Table" menu, go to "Gridline" and you can either show "Gridlines" to see the border or "Hide Gridlines." It's easier to use the formatting function. Go to "Format," click on "Border and Shading" click "None" on the border. This will make the table grey. It will be visible to you on the screen, but if you print the document, it will not show the gridlines.

This table hides the gridlines
(Will not print gridlines)

Merge cells to give the table a different look

Column 1, 2 and 3 are merged into one cell by highlighting all the cells and from the "Table" menu, simply by clicking on "Merge Cell." To add visual effect to this table, you can add color by formatting it. Go to the "Format" menu, in "Border and Shading," go to "Shading" and pick the desired color. You can also find the "Border and Shading" in the "Table" menu under "Table Properties."

<table>
<tr><th colspan="3">Merged Cells</th></tr>
<tr><td></td><td></td><td></td></tr>
<tr><td></td><td></td><td></td></tr>
<tr><td></td><td></td><td></td></tr>
</table>

Split cell

Pick a cell and create multiple columns or rows from that cell. Highlight the area and go to "Table" split cell. This cell has 2 columns and 1 row. Again, to add visual, you can use "Border and Shading."

<table>
<tr><td></td><td></td><td></td><td></td></tr>
<tr><td colspan="2"></td><td></td><td></td></tr>
<tr><td colspan="2"></td><td></td><td></td></tr>
</table>

Split table

You can divide your table by using this format or you can divide by using the command "CTRL Enter." The other alternative is to highlight the area that should be divided and go to "Table," and split the desired area.

Sort data

This command is used to sort columns alphabetically or numerically, either using the header or not. You can sort ascending or descending, i.e. "1, 2, 3" or "3, 2, 1."

If you have a list of names you wish to sort, just highlight the area, go to "Sort" and choose by "Column" or "Paragraph," then using a header "Descending" or "Ascending."

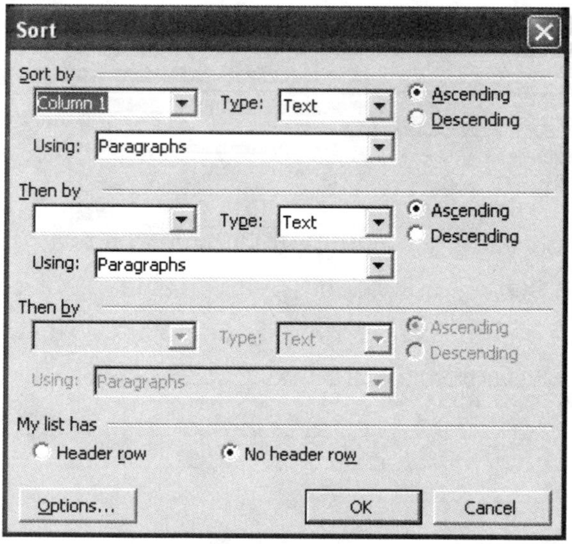

Table properties

The best use of this command is to position your table on the screen. When the table is not positioned properly, it does not look professional. If you want to center the table to make the page look professional, you need to highlight the table and go to "Table AutoFormat" and pick "Center."

The second option is to use the "Border and Shading" at the bottom of the grid. This will enable you to style your table, add color and various border styles, etc., instead of having a boring table you can use "Table AutoFormat" to add dimensions to your table. Enclosed are some samples of "Table AutoFormat" options:

	Jan	Feb	Mar	Total
East	7	7	5	19
West	6	4	7	17
South	8	7	9	24
Total	21	18	21	60

	Jan	**Feb**	**Mar**	**Total**
East	7	7	5	19
West	6	4	7	17
South	8	7	9	24
Total	**21**	**18**	**21**	**60**

	JAN	**FEB**	**MAR**	**TOTAL**
East	7	7	5	19
West	6	4	7	17
South	8	7	9	24
Total	**21**	**18**	**21**	**60**

Create a table formatted manually

You can also create interest to a table manually. Enclosed is a table that was manually arranged to create interest. To achieve this table below, the following steps were taken:

Click on "Table" Insert table, 3 columns and 5 rows. The first 3 rows were merged to give a "Table Title." To color the "Table Title" grid, highlight the area of "Table Title" from the "Format" menu, "Border and Shading" was picked.

To pick a style, go the "Style" menu and pick the desired style. This one was chosen from the drop down menu in "Style." To obtain the gray color, go to "Shading," pick a shade of gray. The white letters were done in "Format" "Font" "Color." The rest of the table was a mix of the columns highlighted in the same border and rows highlighted and formatted with the generic border.

TABLE TITLE		

8. WINDOW

To view documents

If you are working with multiple documents, you can navigate back and forth with multiple windows with this function.

A cool function on “Window” lets you view two windows side by side by splitting the screen into two different screens. However, if you have more than two documents that you are working with, it will split the windows in as many windows as are open in Word.

You can see all the documents that are open in Word. You can click on the document to go from one document to the next.

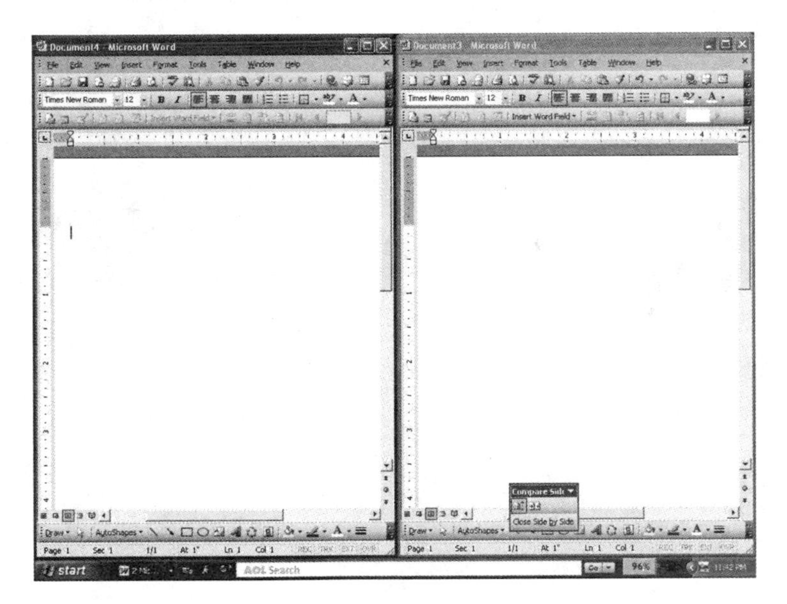

9. HELP

To find information on how to use the functions you can navigate through the "Table of Contents"

If you are unsure about how to use a command, bring down the "Help" menu and you can either use the table of contents or type what you need help with. The directions will appear on the screen. When in doubt, use "Help." (Shortcut: F1)

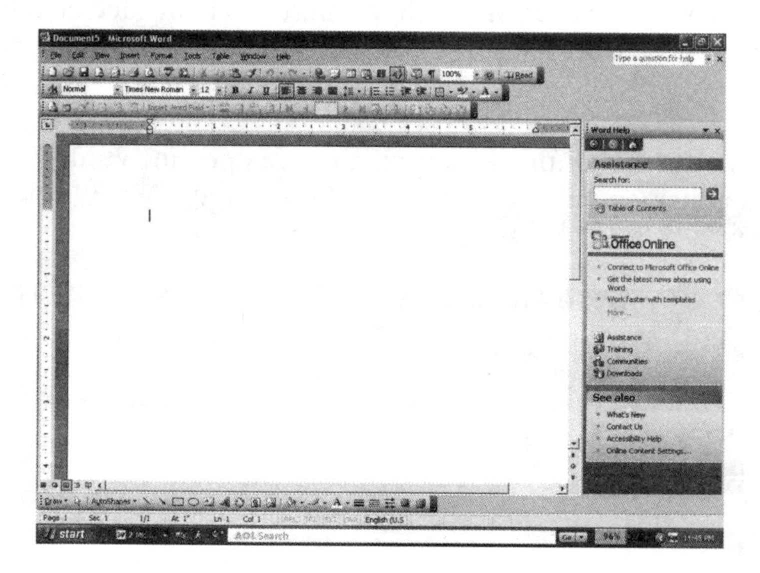

MICROSOFT WINDOWS SHORTCUTS

ACTION	KEYS
Bold	CTRL + B
Copy	CTRL + C
Fonts	CTRL + D
Italics	CTRL + I
Launch Help	Windows Key F1
Paste	CTRL + V
Print	CTRL + P
Redo	CTRL + Y
Save	CTRL + S
Select All Items	CTRL + A
Spell Check	F7
Underline	CTRL + U
Undo	CTRL + Z
When In Doubt	Esc = Escape
Font Size To Normal	CTRL + Shift + N
Open A Document	CTRL + O
Close Window	CTRL + F4
Alignment Right	CTRL + R

Quick Key Strokes - Press SHIFT+ Any Of The Following Keystrokes To Select Text	
ACTION	KEYS
LEFT ARROW	Left one character at a time
RIGHT ARROW	Right one character at a time
DOWN ARROW	Down one line at a time
UP ARROW	Up one line at a time
CTRL+ LEFT ARROW	Left one word at a time
CTRL+ RIGHT ARROW	Right one word at a time
HOME	To the beginning of the current line of text
END	To the end of the current line of text
CTRL+HOME	To the beginning of the document
CTRL+END	To the end of the document
PAGE UP	Up one full screen
PAGE DOWN	Down one full screen
CTRL+PAGE UP	To the beginning of the previous page
CTRL+PAGE DOWN	To the beginning of the next page

What I learned from this chapter:

NOTES

Using Outlook

Outlook is the ultimate organizer. It is a great multitasking tool to help you:

- Send email
- Get organized
- Schedule meetings
- Create and maintain a database of contacts of clients, co-workers and maybe personal friends
- Write notes on specific items, etc.

In order to fully benefit from the great use of Outlook, it must be open every day for the calendar to work efficiently and advise you of scheduled appointments, meetings, etc. Used properly in conjunction with a PDA, Outlook is an organizing tool that will not fail you.

Your IT department will set up your email address in Outlook. Your email address will be determined by how the computer person sets up email addresses in the company. Some companies use first initial and last name. Others use different combinations to create email addresses for their employees.

It is wise to create an alternate email account on one of the free email provider sites such as: Yahoo, Gmail, AOL or Hotmail. If your company email is down, you can use one of them. You should also keep a copy of your address book in this secondary email address. It will come in handy should you need to use that account.

Before using Outlook setting up various commands after establishing an email account will make you a more organized employee.

Set up Signatures for your email

From the "Tools" menu, go to "Options." Choose "Mail Format"; at the bottom of the page choose "Signatures" or "Signature Picker." Click on "Signatures." Click on "New."

Start with a blank signature (if you are setting up for the first time.) Title your signature. Using your first name is recommended. You can have multiple signatures. Enter your information in the box. I don't suggest using the company logo because it takes a lot of space on your system each time you send an email out. Also, if a recipient does not have high speed Internet, uploading the logo will take time.

You can also change the font and the alignment. To change the font, you must pick the format on the first line to show "Microsoft Outlook Rich Text." Your signature should include the following:

- Name
- Title
- Department (optional)
- Company Name
- Telephone
- Fax
- Email address
- Company web address.

Set spelling for email

From the "Tools" menu, go to "Options." Select "Spelling" at the bottom of the "Spelling" window, click on "Always check for spelling before sending."

Options

Preferences | Mail Setup | Mail Format | Spelling | Security | Other

General options

- [x] Always suggest replacements for misspelled words
- [x] Always check spelling before sending
- [ ] Ignore words in UPPERCASE
- [ ] Ignore words with numbers
- [x] Ignore original message text in reply or forward
- [x] Use AutoCorrect when Word isn't the e-mail editor

AutoCorrect Options...

Edit custom dictionary

Add, change, or remove words from your custom dictionary.

Edit...

International dictionaries

Choose which dictionary to use when checking your spelling.

Language: English (U.S.)

OK | Cancel | Apply

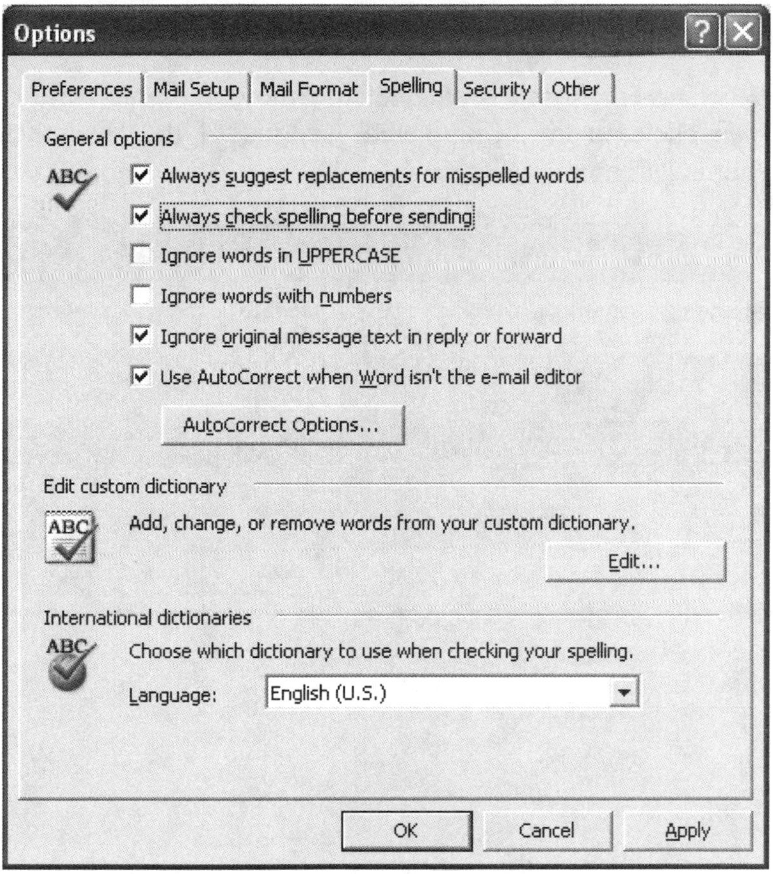

Set up a reminder to follow-up on an email

You can read an email and set up a reminder or a flag of "things to do" for to the email at a later date. To set up a "Flag," while the email is open, go to "Actions." Select "Follow-Up," then "Add Reminders." This will allow you to set a date when you should follow-up on the email.

When an email task is completed, follow the same pattern, then click on the "Completed" section of the "Delete a Reminder" box.

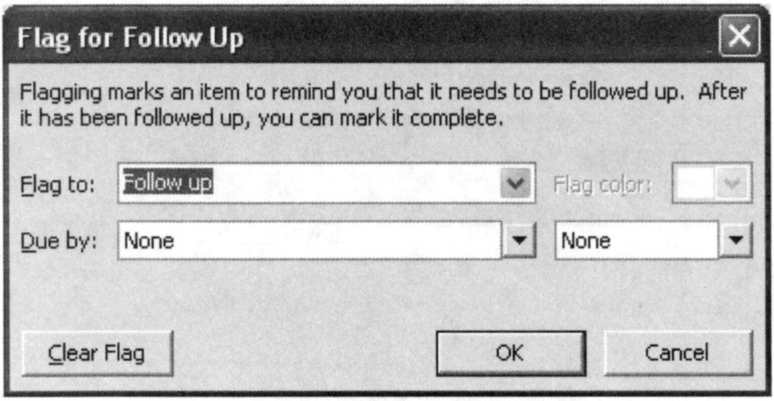

Flag for Follow Up

Flagging marks an item to remind you that it needs to be followed up. After it has been followed up, you can mark it complete.

Flag to: Follow up Flag color:

Due by: None None

Clear Flag OK Cancel

Using the calendar in Outlook to get organized

In the calendar, you can schedule:

- An appointment: activity that involves you
- A meeting: involves others
- An event: may involve anyone but does not block time from your schedule.

The enclosed calendar view shows this display when you click on "1-Day." It allows you to see the "1-Day" page date with the two-month calendar on the right side of the screen along with the task screen. If the calendar does not show, adjust the screen with the mouse and curser by making the "1-Day" view smaller.

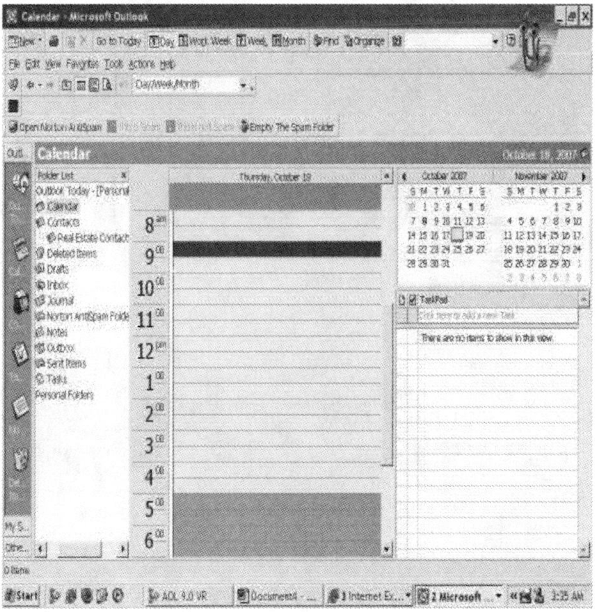

Using the date navigator

Once the calendar is open it will display the choices of a "Day," "Week" or "Month" view. To switch different views use the navigator. The date navigator (picture enclosed) allows you to see a closer view of how to navigate from one day to an entire month on the calendar.

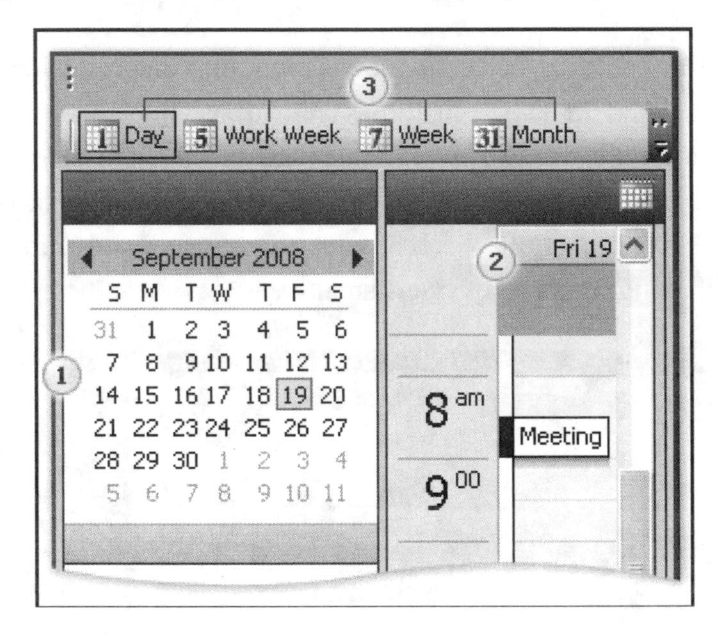

Scheduling a meeting, task or appointment

To enter a task, meeting or appointment, click on the date of the function and pick the time. A dialog box will open. You can name the task, appointment or meeting, select the date, time and/or duration of the task/meeting. You can also add notes.

The coolest tool is the "Reminder." You can set a time for Outlook to remind you of the task to be performed. This is only valuable if Outlook is always open when you are at work. Also, remember to synchronize with a PDA when outside of the office.

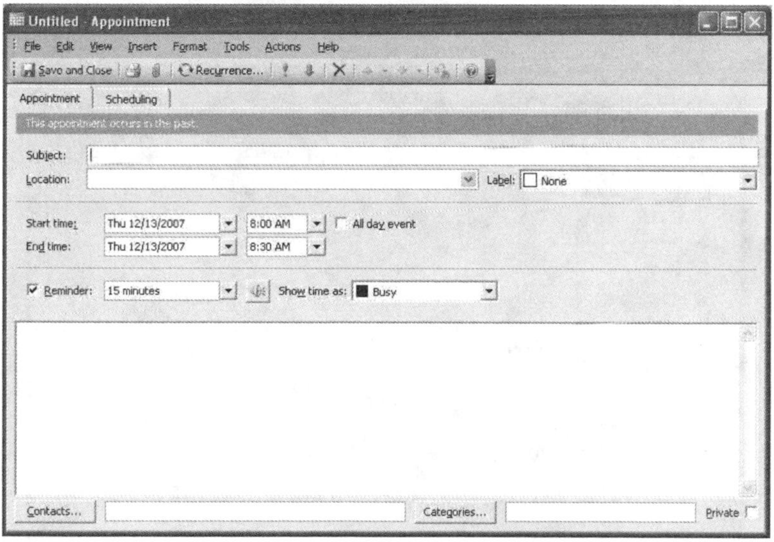

Schedule a recurrent meeting, appointment or task

Outlook will block your time schedule and avoid scheduling conflicts in your calendar. You can also set up an action that occurs frequently either daily, weekly or monthly, bi-weekly or bi-monthly. To achieve this, click on "Calendar," follow the same pattern to schedule a meeting, appointment or event. In the appointment grid, enter the appointment, and then on the top find the "Recurrence" button.

When you click on "Recurrence," another window will open. Pick the "Recurrence" pattern: day, time, the "Start date" and the "End Date." You can also select a date to end the recurrence or select a specific number of recurrences.

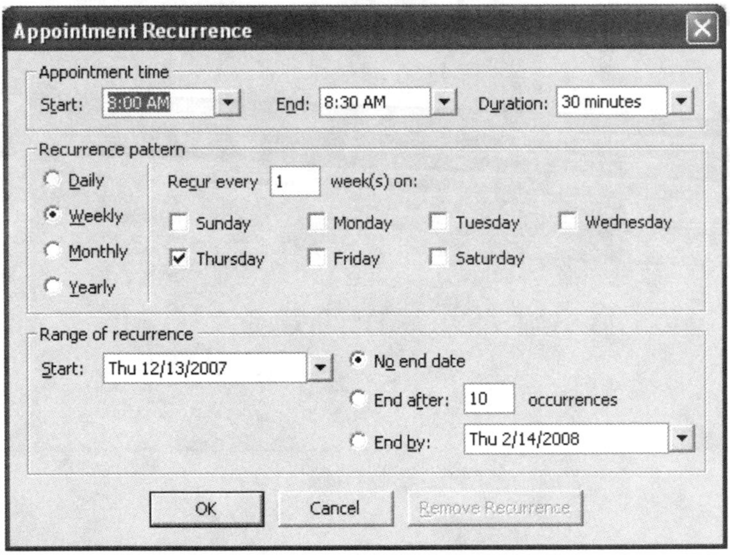

Working with contacts

Outlook is a great instrument to keep your contacts organized. You can also create various folders to save your contacts by filing them according to your needs. You can create a contact subfolder called "Personal Contacts," another one called "Business Contacts," and one named "Vendors." In each contact file, you can put name, contact info and add notes. You can also flag a contact if you have to call a contact on a specific date. This program is used as a sales tool. It is a great way to build a database, follow-up with calls, insert notes, etc.

To create a new contact folder, go to "Contacts," right click and choose "New Folder," rename the folder as needed, i.e. "Vendors:"

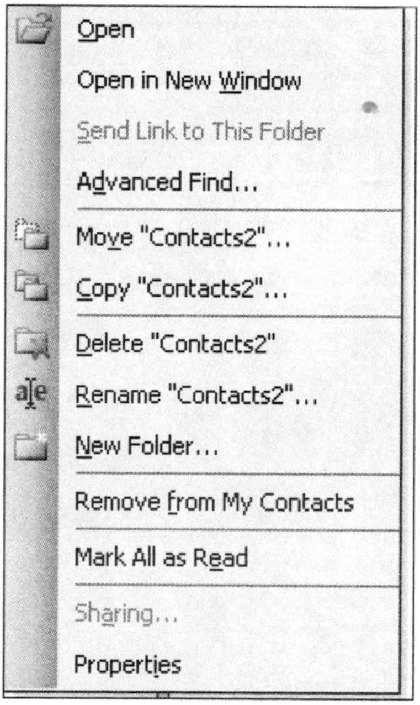

To create a new contact, click on “File,” click on “New Contact” or just click on the “New” icon on the toolbar and enter the information for the new contact.

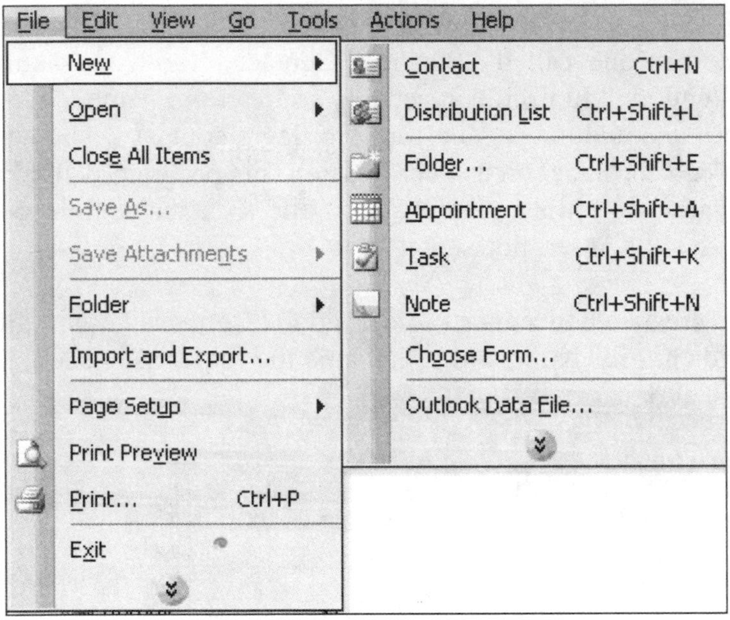

To put a reminder on a contact, open the contact and click on the “Flag” to add a reminder date on the flag. To enter the date, click on “Due By” and click on “Date and Time.”

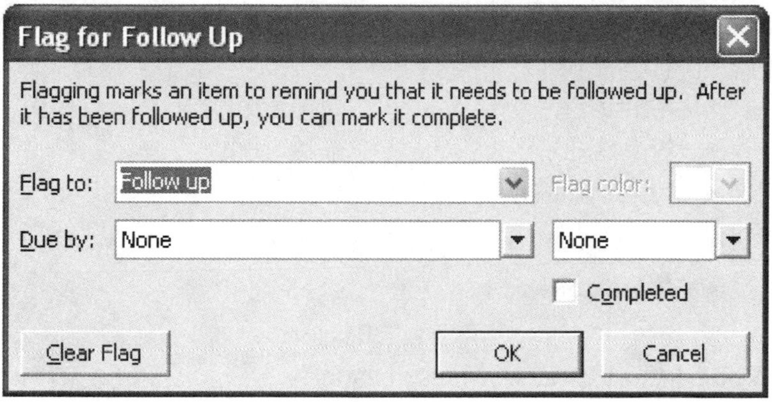

Because you can lose access to your computer in case of emergencies, it is recommended to print your contacts once a while. Having your contacts on paper is a great asset should you not have access to your computer.

How to work with task lists

You can create a "To do List" or a "Task" in Outlook. What's cool is the ability to enter fields in the following headers:

- "Subject"
- "Status"
- "Due Date"
- "% Complete"
- "Categories"

You can sort by any of these headers.

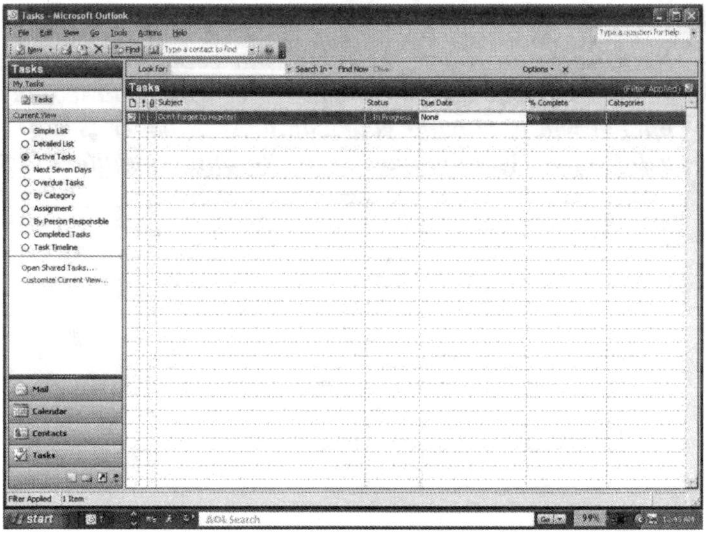

You can arrange and sort your tasks by "Subject," "Date Due" (which becomes a reminder,) "% Completed" and "Categories."

MICROSOFT OUTLOOK SHORTCUTS

ACTION	**KEYS**
Create Email	CTRL – Shift - M
Reply to Selected Email	CTRL – R
Forward Selected Email	CTRL – F
Save Draft of Email	CTRL – S
Create Flag or Follow-Up	CTRL – Shift – G
Create Contact	CTRL – Shift – C
Open Address Book	CTRL – Shift – B
Create Task	CTRL – Shift – K
Assign Task Category	Alt – G
Save and Close Task	Alt – S
Create Appointment	CTRL – Shift – A
Create Meeting Request	CTRL – Shift – Q
Create Note	CTRL – Shift – N
Open Selected Item	Enter
Close Window	Esc = Escape

Inspirational Quote

"He is wise who knows the sources of knowledge – who knows who has written and where it is to be found."

- A. A. Hodge

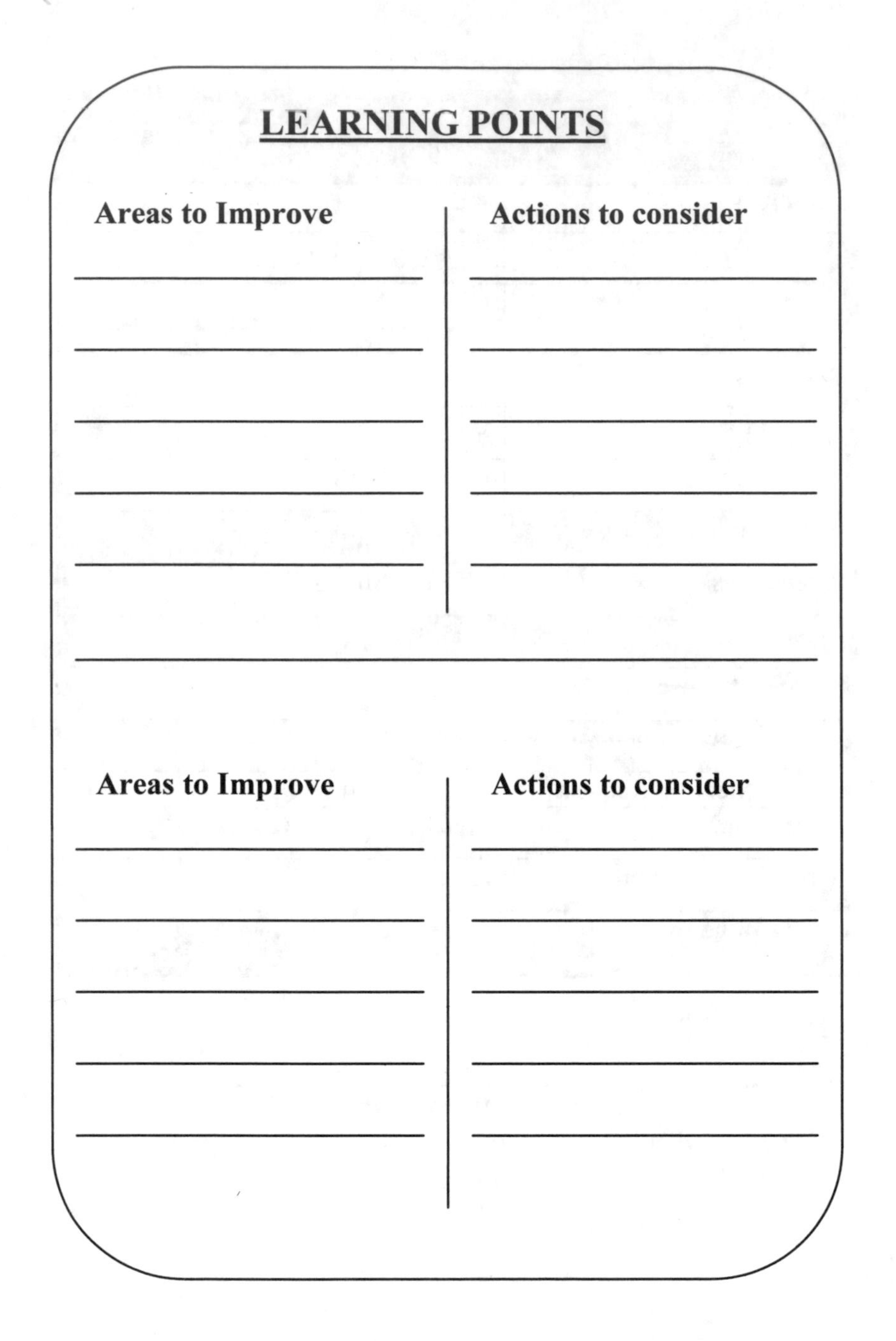
LEARNING POINTS
Areas to Improve
Actions to consider
Areas to Improve
Actions to consider

What I learned from this chapter:

NOTES

CHAPTER 8

SEARCHING FOR A TEMPORARY EMPLOYEE

One of the duties of the administrative employee is to assist in the search for full-time and temporary employees. This chapter will offer guidelines to find temporary help.

In your position as an Administrative Assistant, many times you will need help. If you are the department assistant, the role of hiring a temporary employee will become a part of your responsibilities. You may be required to contact a temporary agency, which is a third-party employer to hire a "temp." A "temp" is someone who works for an employment agency. The recruiting agency leases the services of the temp to a company for a fee. The agency performs all the pre-screening, testing, background check, etc. They have a pool of workers trained, competent and ready to work.

A full-time employee hired through an employment agency will cost a premium. A fee is usually paid to the agency. However, if the employee is not hired permanently right away, the agency collects a fee for the duration of the short-term contract. If the temp is hired full-time after three months, the fee for hiring the employee on a full-time basis is waived. When part-time or temporary employment is contracted, only a fixed hourly rate is paid to the agency.

Because the temp works for an agency, your company does not have to go through the lengthy hiring procedures. It takes three weeks to a month before a new employee can start work (because of HR employment procedures) while a temp is ready to work the next day.

A temp is a competent, skilled and able worker who is in between jobs. This wonderful creature will come to your office and work his or her magic. You will be amazed at the capacity and ability of the temp to adapt to your environment. In no time, the temp will organize your office and get things rolling. The temp is usually hired to put out fires in the office and for an emergency replacement on a short a basis.

The employment agencies do a great job at selecting competent candidates. They have the tools required to test the candidates. They use various tests to determine and examine the skills and abilities of the candidates.

Usually the recruiting agencies test for various skills including the use of computer programs. They test for:

- Word
- Excel
- Powerpoint
- Accounting softwares: such as Peachtree, Quickbooks, etc.
- Grammar
- Spelling
- Math
- Customer service skills.

Hiring employees directly as a contractor

If your company finds a suitable worker and wants to bypass the pre-employment procedures or use the services of a recruiting agency, a contract can be drafted and the employcc can be hired as a contractor. In this case the contractor will be paid upon the submission of an invoice. That will allow the person to start employment immediately. The contractor, however, is not an employee. He/she will have to take care of paying the income taxes directly to the IRS.

Finding a Temporary Agency

If you work for a corporation, the HR department will provide you with the help required for temporary replacement. If you work for a small company, you may consult the Internet for an agency. There are a host of employment agencies that have a pool of employees ready to start work with minimal notice.

Preparing for temporary personnel at time of replacement:

- Assess the work that needs to be done. Often, you need additional help for work that has been accumulating

- If the worker is replacing someone on leave or out sick, a job description of the position is required. If one is not available, create one before the person leaves, if possible

- Prepare a portfolio for the newcomer, including: information about the company, its philosophy and/or mission statement. A listing of products and/or services of the corporation, list of employees in the department. You will need to specify which employee(s) the temp will assist

- It might be beneficial for the temp to participate in your regular orientation program. Remember, that person will be in contact with customers who do business with the company and the more informed the person will be, the better the performance of the worker will be.

You found a temp. Now, how do you integrate that person into your company? Refer to the orientation section of the book or as follows:

- Introduce the temporary personnel to everyone, if possible in their workspace. It will help the person visualize the workers in their location and will let them know where to go to find the person, if needed. By introducing the employee to everyone, it will make getting to know the other employees and the transition into the department easier. Remember to mention the specific individuals that temp will be working for including their titles

- Give the new temporary member of the staff a tour of the office, including the location of supplies. Provide a demonstration of the operation of the equipment such as: the telephone system, the photocopy and fax machines. If you use codes to access office machines, remember to give the temp all necessary codes

- Review the job description of the position with the temporary employee

- Explain the work schedule i.e. time in and out, breaks and lunch time. Also, give a highlight of the company policies.

Inspirational Quote

"Life is the continuous adjustment of internal relations to external relations."

--Herbert Spencer

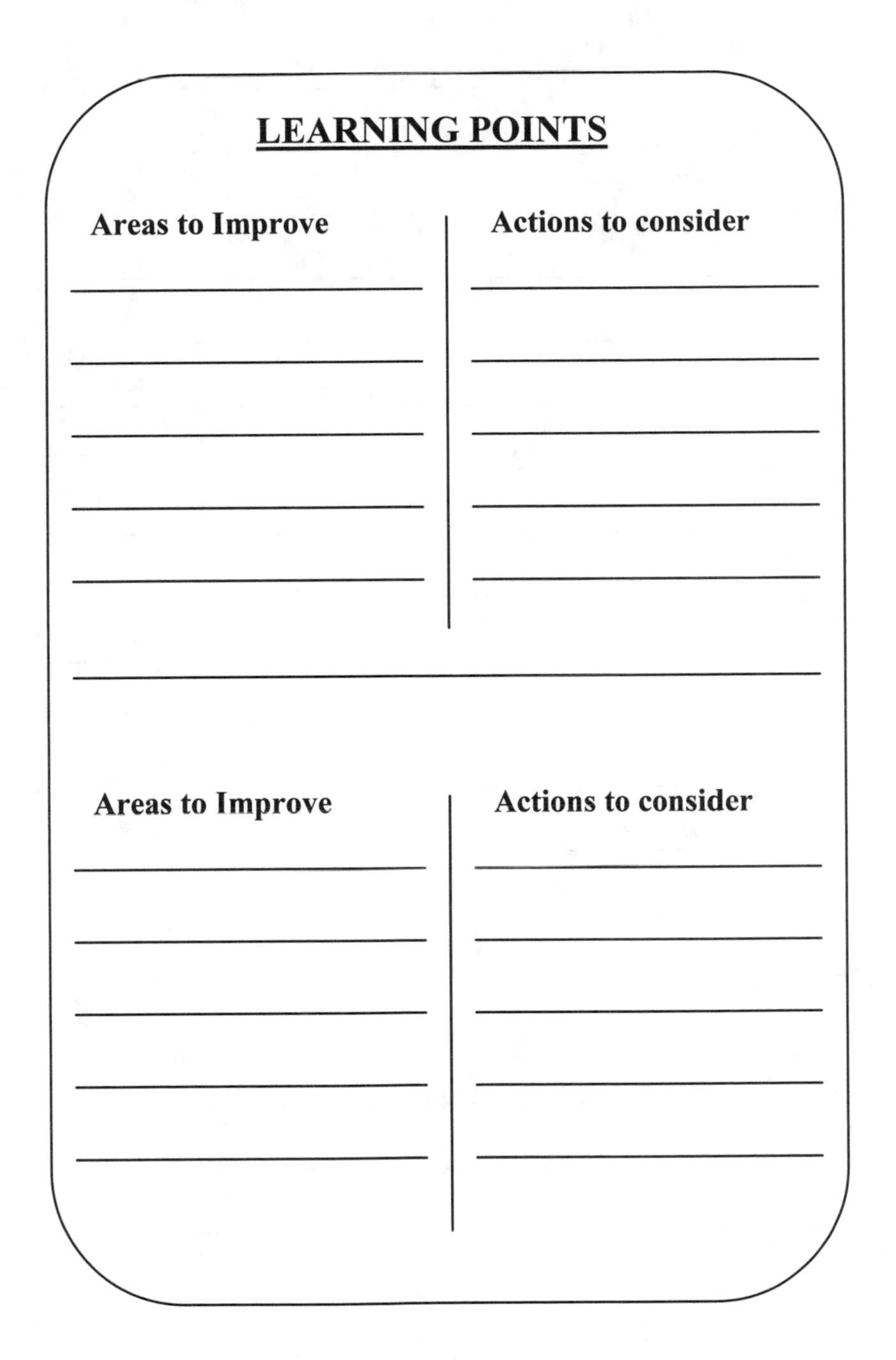
LEARNING POINTS
Areas to Improve
Actions to consider
Areas to Improve
Actions to consider

What I learned from this chapter:

NOTES

CHAPTER 9

LOOKING FOR WORK

To get a job, this segment covers the different ways to land a position, how to create and upgrade one's resume and prepare for a job interview.

- Creating or upgrading a resume
- Preparing for a job interview
- Working for a temporary agency.

A Guide to Writing Your Resume

The word "resumé" means "summary" in French. Writing your resume or curriculum vitae (C.V. for short) is nothing more than a short compilation of summaries of your job descriptions. Everything you do when working is material for your resume. A resume is also a summary of your education and work experience. It should be well written.

Remember that you are judged by your written word. There is no room for mistakes, misspelled words, inaccurate information, etc. This document must portray you in your best light. Your resume can get or lose the job for you.

The resume must be clear, concise and not contain any errors. It is recommended to have the resume reviewed by as many people as possible. Preferably by people who have an excellent command of the English language. The composition of a phrase in French, Spanish and most foreign languages may not make sense in English. Always have someone you trust, and who is a professional, review your resume and your cover letter before sending them.

The resume is also a way to sell yourself and make a great first impression. You won't have another opportunity to make a good impression. Along with the resume is a cover letter. A good cover letter will get your resume read. It's a great introduction and a complement to your resume.

Years ago, we had one resume that covered everything and was sent for all applications for employment. A current trend is to customize your resume to the position advertised by using the terms used on the ad. It ensures that your resume is not overlooked for the position.

Keep the resume to one page. If you want a more detailed resume, make a more detailed resume and bring it with you to the interview. Giving more than one page to a prospective employer going through multiple resumes will ensure that yours is left behind.

The resume must contain

Your personal information:

- Your name: in bigger font than anything else on the resume
- Address: residence or mailing
- Telephone: your cellular and home phone. If you don't have a phone, use someone's phone where you can be reached
- Email: If you have a funny email like "sexygirl69@whatever.com," it is recommended that a more professional email containing your first or last name be created on Gmail, Hotmail, Yahoo, AOL, etc.

Career Goals or Professional Objective:

- A brief summary of your wish list, or expectations, for a position

Skills:

- A segment about your special skills. Include your computer skills and your level of computer literacy (if you have a Microsoft Office User Specialist (MOUS) certification provide the details of the certification,) numbers of words typed per minute (WPM), special accomplishments, any languages written and/or spoken, internships, fellowships, military service, etc. Many employers value individuals from the military because of their training and work ethics

Education:
- Your education: starting with your most recent graduation or certification

Employment History:
- Start with your current or most recent position
- Each position should be bullet pointed starting with the "From Date" to "End Date," name of company and your title

References:
- Available, or furnished, on request

In Conclusion:
- The resume should end with your hobbies, trade association memberships, extra-curricular activities or achievements.

RESUME CHEAT SHEET A-M	
Accomplished	Documented
Acquired	Edited
Administered	Emphasized
Advised	Ensured
Allocated	Established
Analyzed	Evaluated
Assisted	Executed
Attended	Expanded
Authored	Facilitated
Balanced	Formulated
Budgeted	Furnished
Built	Generated
Compiled	Guaranteed
Completed	Guided
Composed	Hired
Computed	Identified
Conceived	Increased
Conducted	Implemented
Contributed	Improved
Cooperated	Informed
Coordinated	Initiated
Created	Investigated
Designed	Issued
Developed	Maintained
Directed	Managed
Distributed	Marketed

RESUME CHEAT SHEET M-Z	
Monitored	Researched
Negotiated	Responsible for
Notified	Restructured
Opened	Reviewed
Operated	Revised
Optimized	Scheduled
Ordered	Served
Organized	Set up
Participated	Solved
Performed	Streamlined
Planned	Structured
Prepared	Submitted
Presented	Succeeded
Produced	Supervised
Proposed	Supplied
Provided	Supported
Publicized	Trained
Published	Tracked
Purchased	Updated
Recommended	Used
Recruited	Utilized
Reduced	Verified
Regulated	Worked
Reported	Wrote
Required	

Preparing for the interview

This part of the book covers one of my ultimate weaknesses: getting a job through the very frustrating process of being interviewed. I am honestly the worst interviewee on the planet. I will just be reporting in this chapter what I have learned from others. Although my interview skills are weak, my work ethics, skills, looking for work and my resume are impeccable. I have always been hired through employment agencies and 99% of the time I have become a full-time employee. Therefore, I love the employment agencies.

With that said, I am a big fan of getting your foot through the door through an agency. The business of employment brokerage is a multi-billion dollar business that has been around for a long time. What I personally like about the agencies is that not only it does it give you the opportunity to find employment quickly, but it also allows you to test-drive the job before accepting a job permanently.

Going to an interview is a very stressful process. What do most people fear most? Public speaking. And being interviewed is almost like public speaking with more scrutiny. The Internet is a very valuable tool to help you prepare for an interview. Many websites are dedicated to providing you with the best interview techniques.

To ease the interview process, it is important to review some of the most asked questions. Practice how to answer these questions and use real life examples to illustrate your answers. If you put enough feeling into your interview, you should nail the job interview.

Your communication should be open-ended. Don't just answer "yes or no." You want to elaborate briefly on your answers. If you offer only yes or no answers, you won't offer your interviewer an insight into your personality and evaluate your work experience.

Always use formal attire when going to an interview. If the environment is casual, you can dress down when you are hired. However, your first impression should be formal. Keep the colors toned down and don't show too much.

Arrive early. You may have to complete an application prior to the interview. By arriving early, you can complete the application in a timely manner. It also gives you an opportunity to practice your employment history and job responsibilities.

Bring copies of your resume and your diplomas and enough copies for the number of people who will interview you if you have a panel interview. Set one aside for yourself. If you have an extended version of your resume and want to use it at the interview, this is your opportunity.

During the interview, maintain eye contact with the person you are answering to while acknowledging the others, if any, in the room. Smile, it helps. Use funny anecdotes when referring to your answers.

Be a good listener. If you don't understand a question, ask for the interviewer to elaborate. Don't cut and don't overextend your answers.

Be graceful under fire. Don't show that you are stressed by the interview. Guess what? Most of the time, the interviewer is also stressed out about interviewing you.

At the end of the interview, take the opportunity to ask some questions relevant to the position.

List of things to bring to the interview:

- Directions to the interview
- Name of your contact
- Telephone number
- Copies of resume
- Diplomas
- Identification and proof of legal status to work in the U.S.
- List of references: remember to confirm with them before using them as a reference.

Enclosed are some sample questions that can arise at an interview:

1. Tell me about yourself
   Be ready to talk about your personal, educational and professional life. You should really be prepared to describe why you chose your career path, your various accomplishments and special skills. Don't be shy about talking about yourself. You may not

have another opportunity to tell them about yourself again

2. What do you know about our company?
3. Why do you want to work for us?
4. Unique qualities and abilities would you bring to the job
5. Strengths and weaknesses
6. How long do you plan to stay with our company? – Where do you see yourself in five years?
7. Tell me a time you failed at something and what you did afterwards to correct it
8. Describe a time you worked on a team project. What was your relative position on the team? – Where you satisfied with your contribution? How could you have been better?
9. Why did you choose your school and course of study?
10. Think back to a situation in which there was a conflict you had to resolve. Tell me how you resolved that conflict.
11. Tell me about a project that you had either at work or school. Describe in detail how you managed it and what was the outcome?
12. What do you do in your spare time?
13. What salary are you expecting?
14. What other types of jobs or companies are you considering?
15. Do you have any questions for us?

If you prepare these questions in your own way, you should be ready for the interview. One of my friends told me about coaching her daughter for an interview. The daughter is a nurse. When asked why she became a nurse? The answer was: "When she was a child, her mother was sick. She wished she could help but couldn't at the time and felt helpless. From that day on she decided to become a nurse so she can gain the knowledge to help sick people."

Another friend noted on the question: "What is your weakness?" She answered: "My weakness is that when I start something, I can't stop, I have to finish it." I told her: "How is that a weakness?" She replied that: "People may not really want to know about your weakness." Therefore, even your weakness must be expressed as a: "strength in disguise."

Looking for employment

There are many reasons why people end up looking for work through an employment agency also referred to as private staffing agencies and recruiting agencies:

- Unhappy with current employment where a work situation is unbearable
- Suddenly lost a job or got laid off and must find work fast
- Re-entering the workforce after being out of the job market for a while

Whatever the reason, you can count on these recruiters to find you employment right away.

To help the job search, enclosed are some systems and tools. Looking for work is a full-time job. Things you need to do:

1) Sign-up and create an on-line resume or search through the local newspapers
2) Create your own website by purchasing yourname.com and include a page that contains your resume. Be careful not to include information that can be used to steal your identity. You can buy a domain at godaddy.com or yahoo.com. This is very cool, but remember that there are costs associated with creating your own website
3) Search for the desired jobs
4) Apply for the jobs
5) Keep track of which jobs you have submitted your resume
6) Modify your resume and cover letters to reflect the position applied for
7) Prepare for the interviews (includes researching information about the company)
8) Look at all the possible questions that can be asked at the interview
9) Follow-up with prospective employers and send thank you notes.

Sounds exhausting? It's not any easier to look for work through employment brokerage firms.

1. You have to register with multiple agencies. This will ensure that you always have employment since the assignments last from one week to many months or full-time
2. Registering with agencies means taking the various tests required to assess your skills and passing them so

you can be assigned to various job opportunities that the agency offers
3. Keep in contact and maintain a relationship with your assigned agent in each agency you sign up with.

Today, the employment agencies are not limited to the administrative professions. Many other workers, such as engineers, laborers, servers, waiters, construction workers, medical professionals, etc. use these agencies to find employment.

Working as a temporary employee

You have now gone through, with a fine toothcomb, the requirements to be listed with a temporary agency and now have a job. Once on the assignment, find out:

- Who will be your direct report?
- Who signs your time sheet?
- Does HR have to review your time sheet?
- Others employees who report to the same manager
- A list of the employees in the department
- A list of employees in the company (depending on the size)
- The name of the HR contact who is your link to the temp agency
- The job description of the previous employee you are replacing
- If possible, the job description of the boss
- The company procedures, rules and regulations.

Pros and cons of working for employment agencies versus working as an employee:

TEMPORARY WORKER	FULL-TIME WORKER
Flexibility of scheduling your own work schedule	Must be available for work on company schedule
Exposed to various industries, workplaces, personalities, people and cultures. Becoming a diversified worker	Consistency of experience that can lead to a specialization in a specific field
New kid on the block gets all the tedious and lousy assignments	Benefit from seniority and can pass tedious work to newer workers
Constantly learning new work and work environments	Job becomes easier. You gain seniority and experience
Agency may or may not collect tax upfront. If hired as a contractor by agency, expenses can be claimed but must pay tax by one-self. Requires organization	Taxes are withheld from paycheck by HR. May not have to pay minimum taxes at end of year
Self-employed and is a sub-contractor for the agency	Employed by a corporation
Harder to get credit when purchasing items such as a: car, house, furniture, credit card, etc.	Easier to obtain credit. May even get it through banks or credit unions that offer incentives to the corporation
No benefits package: - No health insurance, must find own insurance - 401 (k) and pension must be self planned - No sick pay - No vacation pay	Benefits package include: - Health insurance - Retirement benefit such as pension or 401 (k) match - Sick pay - Paid vacation
Flexibility to take vacation anytime without pay	Must plan vacation based on company needs but with pay
No pay between assignments	Always have salary and pay

You got the job, now what? Keeping yourself busy is the best way to obtain a full-time position. It will show that you have initiative and that you are mature and responsible.

What you **can't** do while on temporary assignment:

- Tarnish the reputation of the agency in any way
- Don't arrive late for work and leave early
- Get into arguments with co-workers
- Accept work directly from the contractor of the agency. If the employer/contractor offers you a position without following the proper hiring procedure through the employment agency, you must decline the offer. This shows a blatant lack of integrity on the part of the contractor. The agency survives on the payment from the contractor. A lot of times the agency gets paid 60-90 days following the assignment. However, you (the worker) still receive your pay every week
- If you are approached by the employer, advise your agent of the request so they know the type of client they are dealing with.

At the end of the assignment, always obtain a reference letter from your direct report. At least get a survey card completed. This will ensure that your consultant will receive feedback on how satisfied your employer was with your performance. Also, ask if they will re-hire you, should the opportunity arise.

Other Duties Performed While on Temporary Assignment

Often times, while working on a temporary assignment, you are not always busy. However, because you are being paid, you should work. Also, the reputation of the employment agency that hired you is at stake. The first step is to request for more work from your boss. If nothing comes up, be creative. Enclosed are some suggestions of things every company can use your help with:

- Clean and organize your work station
- Create a list of the files in the filing system
- Create new labels for the files
- Help others in your department
- Update the list of employees in your department
- If your company is small and does not have an equipment inventory created by the financial managers. Create an inventory of the equipment owned by the company
- Create files for all service contracts for the company.

Is your department expanding? Are you moving? Are you working for a start-up company? Enclosed are some things you may need to do or order to transition into your new place:

- Contact leasing companies to find the space to establish the office Once a location has been selected, coordinate the move to set up the office
- Order and arrange for delivery and installation of all furniture and equipment needed:
- Desks
- Chairs
- Filing cabinets
- Computers
- Telephone
- Fax
- If setting up a big company, leasing one or more copy machines may be a better alternative
- Ensure that the office is functional and that the filing system is set up
- Create a list of contacts for all the employees, outside employees, vendors, etc.
- Print business cards, letterheads and envelopes
- Order toll-free number
- Develop fax cover sheet templates for all employees
- Develop filing system
- Hire new employees. The use of temp agencies is strongly recommended until the company is stable.

If you run out of business cards, make some

If you move, you may need to make some business cards until the printer can complete your order. To make the cards:

.

- Purchase a box of cards at any office supply store
- Use the company logo to create your card
- Reduce the size of the logo
- Use the regular company business card layout.

To print the cards

- Go to "Tools," "Envelopes and Labels," and pick the "Label" drop down menu. Pick the card number as indicated on the card box purchased.
- Select "New Documents" to insert the "Fonts." If you desire, you may create several layouts of the card and choose your favorite.

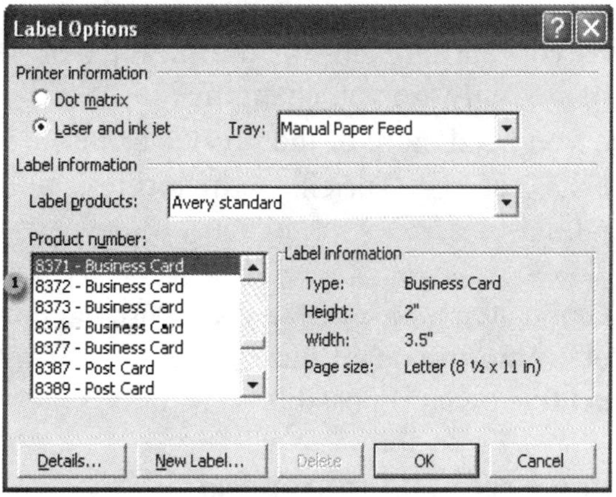

Remember to include the following on your card:

- Company logo
- Company Name
- Address
- Telephone number
- Toll free number (if there is one)
- Fax number
- Email address
- Company Website address.

If your company does not have a procedure for contract requests, call for a bid and/or request for proposal. These are used to purchase equipment and service. In order to obtain the best quality/price ratio, it is recommended that such a request be issued and forwarded to various vendors (four to five should be sufficient.)

The first step is to assess the current needs:

- Are you currently using the product or service? If you are, why are you changing?
- Do you need more of the service or less?
- Verify current pricing, quantities and service contract.

The second step is to analyze the future needs:

- Determine the quantities that will be needed in the next five years if possible.

Creating a request for proposal

Provide an overview of the company, its products or services. Copies of your marketing brochures should be included. Insert a reception confirmation return card to ensure that the recipient received your request. A deadline to return a proposal must be given. If your company does business nationwide, find a company that does the same. This list can be used for any product ordered. It can serve as a guideline for ordering:

- Quantities per product
- Delivery
- Transport: ship to address
- Invoicing: bill to address

- Shipping costs (included or not included)
- Location of where equipment/service will be used
- Insurance (security)
- Measurements
- Safety issues
- Government regulations
- Deadline for implementation
- Product/service
- Support
- Service contract
- Evaluate the vendors and location
- Do they offer service nationwide?
- Compare prices while considering all criteria
- Assess vendor's ability to deliver the product quickly on short notice and their level of customer service.

Inspirational Quote

"If you don't ask, you don't get."
--Mahatma Gandhi

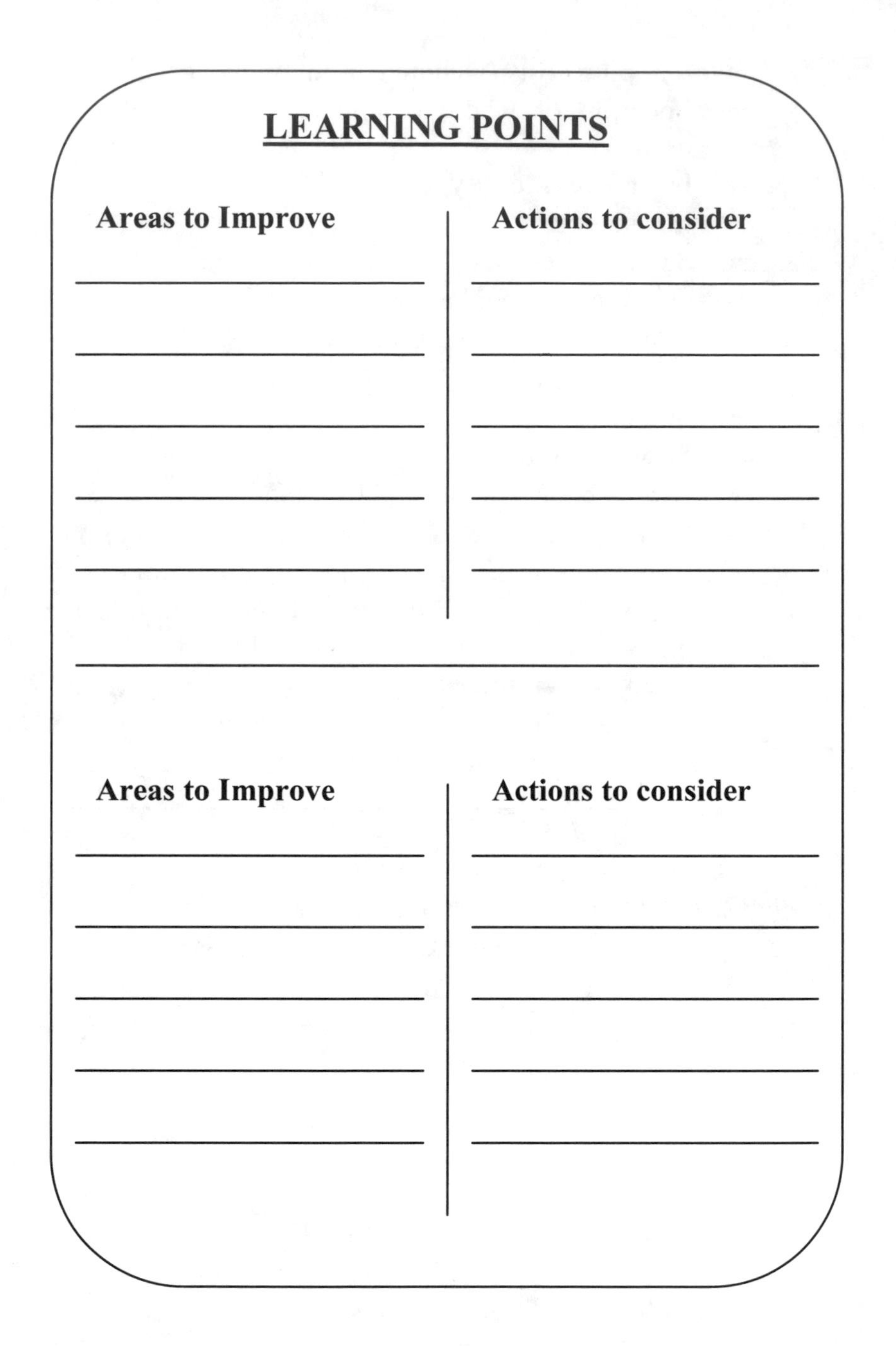
LEARNING POINTS
Areas to Improve
Actions to consider
Areas to Improve
Actions to consider

What I learned from this chapter:

NOTES

CHAPTER 10

COMPANY ORIENTATION

Since the Administrative Assistant is sometimes involved in the hiring process, this chapter covers the steps required when hiring a new employee. This chapter will also outline the steps to prepare for a newly hired worker.

When a new employee starts, the Human Resources Department of the company should have an orientation session with the employee. Some big corporations have scheduled orientation sessions that last for hours.

After the decision is made to hire the new employee and the employee has accepted the offer, the department employees should be advised of the information about the new employee. The company orientation should include the following:

NEW EMPLOYEE INFO
• Name of the new employee • Who the new employee replaces • What will be the new employee's job description • Who will the new employee report to?

Before the new the employee arrives, the Administrative Assistant or the Human resources should provide the new employee information about:

PRE-EMPLOYMENT ACTIVITIES
• The name and title of the supervisor • A job description • Instructions for first day and week • Time and location of employment • Company policy for parking (if available) • Company dress code • Work schedule, including lunch break and other breaks • Inform MIS personnel of the new employee so they can create email account and set up a computer system for the new worker.

When the new employee starts:

EMPLOYEE INTRODUCTION
• Meet with supervisor (and others as appropriate) for office orientation • Meet with company Human Resources Services • Tour the building and immediate areas • Introduce the employee to department employees and any other employees that will have contact with the new recruit • Meet with colleagues and support staff.

INFORMATION TECHNOLOGY ACTIVITIES
• Meet with MIS personnel for computer assistance to create an email account and set up computer system for new worker (if not done yet) • Hardware: turning on, backing up, printing, shutting down, etc. • Software: systems used, company intranet, Internet access, e-mail, etc. - as needed.

LOGISTICS

- How to use the telephone
- How to answer the telephone
- Set up work-space
- Office organization (files location and office supplies cabinet)
- Handling incoming and outgoing mail
- Where to store personal belongings
- Restrooms
- Cafeteria and or/kitchen areas
- Copy machines: how to use, codes for photocopiers (if needed,) refilling paper supply and policies about number of copies and making personal copies
- Fax machines.

COMPANY POLICY

- Review the "Policy and Procedures" manual given to the employee
- Complete all necessary paperwork
- Review the benefits package including insurance, retirement plan, tuition reimbursement, etc.
- Review the job description as it applies to the position
- Paid holidays, vacation and sick time
- Explain evaluation timeline and process

- Office goals and objectives
- Travel and reimbursement (especially for business travelers)
- Company credit card
- Get company ID and/or security card (if required)
- Get company parking permit (if appropriate)
- Shutting down at the end of the day: lights, telephones, doors, computer, etc.

After all these areas are covered, the new employee is ready to start the training. The supervisor should not travel nor be absent for long periods at the beginning and should be available to answer questions.

Inspirational Quote
"Never be afraid to do something new. Remember, amateurs built the ark; professionals built the titanic."
Anonymous

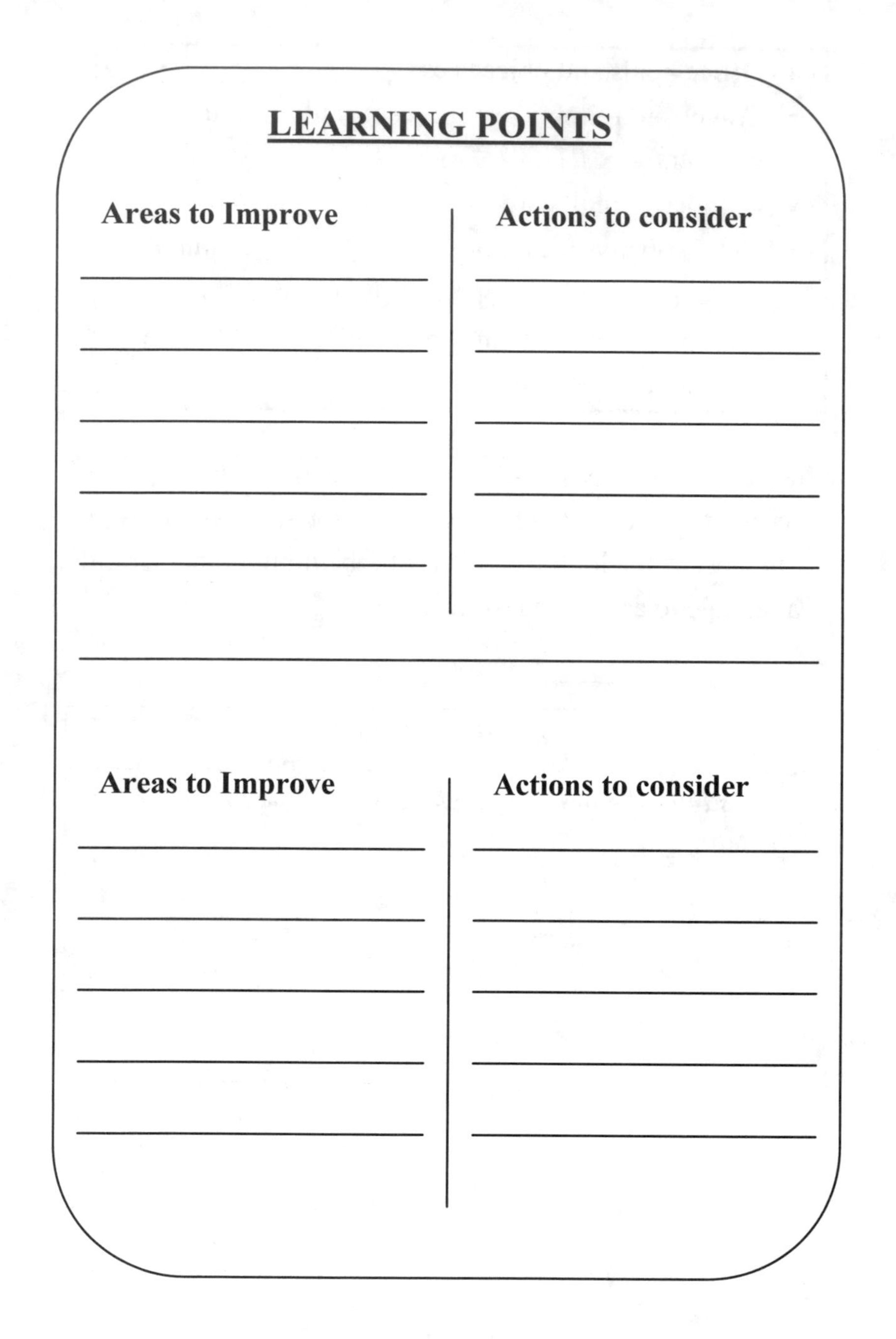
LEARNING POINTS
Areas to Improve
Actions to consider
Areas to Improve
Actions to consider

What I learned from this chapter:

NOTES

CHAPTER 11

LEAVING YOUR JOB

When leaving your job, there are steps to be taken to ensure that you follow a certain protocol. This will enable you to obtain references and maintain good relations with your employer.

- Protocol to resign from your job
- Announce your departure properly
- Items to consider when leaving your job.

Steps to follow when leaving your job

There are many reasons why you may leave your job. Whether you are moving to better opportunities or are just unhappy with your current employment, you should resign from your position in the most ethical way. The reasons for following proper protocol when leaving your job are:

- To create an environment that will make your transition smoother. Since you will have to give a certain amount of notice. Two weeks is the norm. You have to work for those two weeks. These will be the longest two weeks of your life if you don't transition properly. If you don't have another position and have a good relationship with the company, you can give more than two weeks so that they can find and train a replacement. This will give you brownie points in the reference department

- To obtain references from your current employer and to maintain a professional relationship with that employer. Remember that your next employer will contact them for references. You have everything to gain by leaving your employment in good terms. Although there are laws that prohibit your Human Resources Department from providing negative information about your performance, you want them to give excellent recommendations about you

- To be fair to your boss. They need time to replace you and it sometimes takes more than two weeks to find a replacement for you. Most of the time your supervisor doesn't have a clue about your day-to-day job and responsibilities. At least not typically.

Once you have made the decision to leave your job, you should:

a) Update your job description. They will need it for your future replacement

b) Prepare a letter of resignation. This letter must include the date you wish to leave the company. Be brief and positive. Thank your employer or supervisor for the opportunity to work for them. Ask them if there is anything you can do to help during the transition and that you are available to train your replacement

c) Approach your boss first to present your resignation. Under no circumstances should you let anyone know of your plans to leave your job before advising your boss. It's not ethical to do so. It makes your boss feel bad if everyone else knows and he or she is not aware of it. Give your boss a copy of your updated job description along with your resignation letter and offer your assistance to train the next employee to replace you

d) Present your resignation to your Human Resource Department, if there is one.

If you are leaving your job and don't have another position secured, there are things you need to consider.

- Will you have enough money to survive?
- Are you entitled to unemployment? If you leave your job just for the sake of leaving your job, you may not be eligible for unemployment
- What about health insurance? Can you continue with your current health insurance coverage through (COBRA.) Congress passed the landmark Consolidated Omnibus Budget Reconciliation Act (COBRA) health benefit provisions in 1986. The law amends the Employee Retirement Income Security Act, the Internal Revenue Code and the Public Health Service Act to provide continuation of group health coverage that otherwise might be terminated. It can be very costly to maintain your COBRA coverage, especially if you have a family
- If you enrolled in your company's retirement plan or 401 (k) plan, you will need to transfer or roll-over your plan to another company's plan or to a private asset management firm. Consult a financial company on this matter
- If you had items that belonged to your employer, you must return them before leaving, i.e. office keys, credit cards, cell phone, etc.
- Company credit cards should be not only returned but take a step further to advise the credit card companies of your intention to leave the company and obtain a letter of annulment from them

canceling and removing your name from the company card.

Many companies will request an exit interview to determine the reasons why you are leaving. They will try to find out if problems with your boss are the reason for you leaving your job. Be diplomatic about how you answer questions concerning your supervisor.

If you plan your departure properly, you will prepare a job description for your position, have a good attitude, even if you are leaving because you don't like your boss or don't get along with that person. You will have an easier transition, a letter of recommendation and maintain a relationship with your employer or manager for future work reference purposes.

Inspirational Quote
"Life is made up of interruptions."
--William S. Gilbert

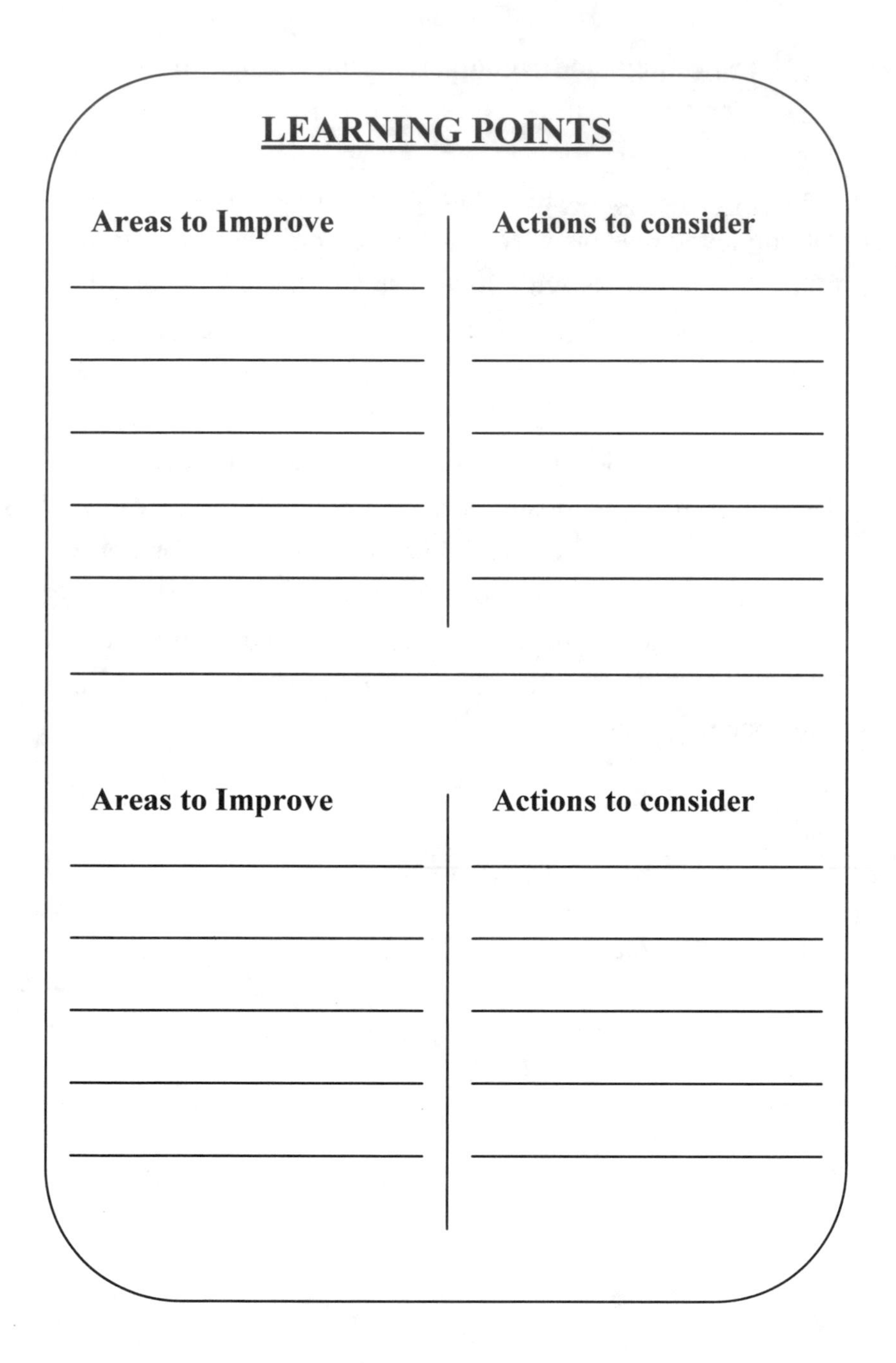
LEARNING POINTS
Areas to Improve
Actions to consider
Areas to Improve
Actions to consider

What I learned from this chapter:

NOTES

CHAPTER 12

WHAT ABOUT ME?
WHAT I CAN DO
WHAT I CAN'T DO

This section of the book is very personal. It caters to the individual on the job, its finances, 401 (k), etc.

As you take care of everybody at work and in your family, there are some recommendations to ensure that you take care of yourself.

What I Can Do

You and your finances: money is extremely important. We work to have it but have a hard time keeping it.

You should pay yourself first. Invest in your company retirement plans such as a 401 (k). Your salary may not allow you to save a lot. However, if you can save what your company will match, you will be ahead of the game. For instance, if you save 5% of your gross salary before tax, your company may match that 5%. Instead of just saving 5% of your salary, you would actually be saving 10%. This money will be invested in your retirement account.

Another great retirement saving tool is the Roth IRA. It is recommended because you can put money without taking the pre-tax exemptions offered by traditional 401 (k) plans. Although you would not enjoy the tax benefits, you can use your money should the need arise without paying a penalty of 10% and tax based on your tax bracket

Removing money from your 401 (k) is only for extreme emergencies. You will be taxed at the rate of approximately 20-30% plus a penalty of 10%.

Pack a lunch: if you earn less than $60,000 a year, you should pack a lunch, make your own coffee and purchase drinks from the supermarket. Spending $10 a day on these items can cost you a lot in the long-term. If you spend $10/day at 4 days per week, that adds up to $160/month.

The yearly total is $1920/year. If you put that in your 401 (k), even if without any interest added to it, it is still a savings of $19,200 for 10 years. Instead, pack a lunch every day except for Fridays, you should order in or go out.

Only invest in items of value or that will have a minimum value in the future: Designer clothing for everyday wear is not recommended on that type of salary. However, you need some good items: A good quality purse, some good shoes and items of clothing are suggested. Custom jewelry is not an investment. However, if you buy gold and diamond pieces, you can turn them into money when you need to. One of my friends recently told me that she pawned her jewelry to pay for school tuition when getting her degree. Now, she buys jewelry at that place.

Credit cards: stay out of debt. You still need to build credit and have credit cards with low interest rate. If you must use your card, your balance should not exceed 30% of the credit limit on the card. You should keep your credit score above 700 middle score. Monitoring one's credit is the best way to maintain your score. This will save you money on interest rates when making big item purchases such as a house, car, appliances, etc.

Create a budget: this is not a profession that offers a grand lifestyle and budgeting becomes crucial. Try to follow a budget and live below your means. Don't buy for the sake of buying. Buy only when you need it. If your budget allows for it, invest a portion of your income. It does not have to be a lot. Big money is piled one, two or ten dollars at a time. All you need is to make a good investment in stocks. Make sure they are on sale in order to make money on a long-term basis. If you are conservative, invest in a CD at your financial institution. Some on-line banks offer a great return on your savings.

Education: most companies have a tuition reimbursement program. You should take advantage of these programs to advance your education. This profession allows you to make money without a degree. However, advancing your education should be a priority. Also, always participate in company training provided on-site or off-site. Remember that the knowledge gained will be yours to keep forever. You can't return the knowledge if you leave your job, but you can use it in your next job.

Enhancing your knowledge in technology is extremely important. Use the company's tuition assistance or allocation to get trained. You will become more efficient on the job and in your personal life.

Get the Microsoft Office User Specialist (MOUS) certification. This certification will guarantee that you will always have a job. You will be more advanced than others in the profession. Technology training is very important.

What I Can't Do

1. **Stealing:** stealing is number one on the "What I can't do list." There is nothing in the office that you can steal that you can't buy at the dollar store. Have you seen some of these stores? Is it worth it to lose your job for something you can purchase for a dollar? Even if it's a pricey item, don't take it. Whatever it is, it's not yours. Also, keep in mind that there may be security cameras set up. They are all over nowadays

2. **Romantic involvements:** never, never, never! You should especially never get involved with your boss. Imagine what happens when Mr. Right becomes Mr. Wrong and you hate each other. He or she is not leaving the job for you. The two of you just have to live as the odd couple

3. **Company credit cards:** this is important - Never attach your social security number to guarantee a credit card or any debt for your employer. If the company goes bankrupt and can't pay the debt, guess who is now in debt? YOU! By signing the card as a user, if the corporation defaults on the debt, you may inherit the debt. Number two: do not purchase personal items on the card. You should always be able to explain what the purchases were for. It is recommended that you keep copies of the invoices for yourself. Should any doubt arise about

purchases made with that credit card, you will have proof of your purchases

4. **Gossip:** you know the old saying “What goes around, comes around.” You don’t know your co-workers until people in high places find out about gossips in the office and interview them. They will sing like birds and leave you in the dark. Never trust your co-workers when it comes to gossiping. Don’t even be present when gossiping is happening. You can be an accessory to gossiping because you were present

5. **Gifts from suppliers:** never accept big gifts from suppliers. You can accept promotional items, a lunch or a small token. However, anything big enough to compromise your involvement with that supplier should be avoided. Also, how can you reprimand a supplier when they don’t perform if you accept their kickbacks?

Inspirational Quote

"Life is like a game of cards. The hand that is dealt you represents determinism; the way you play it is free will."
--Jarawala Nehru

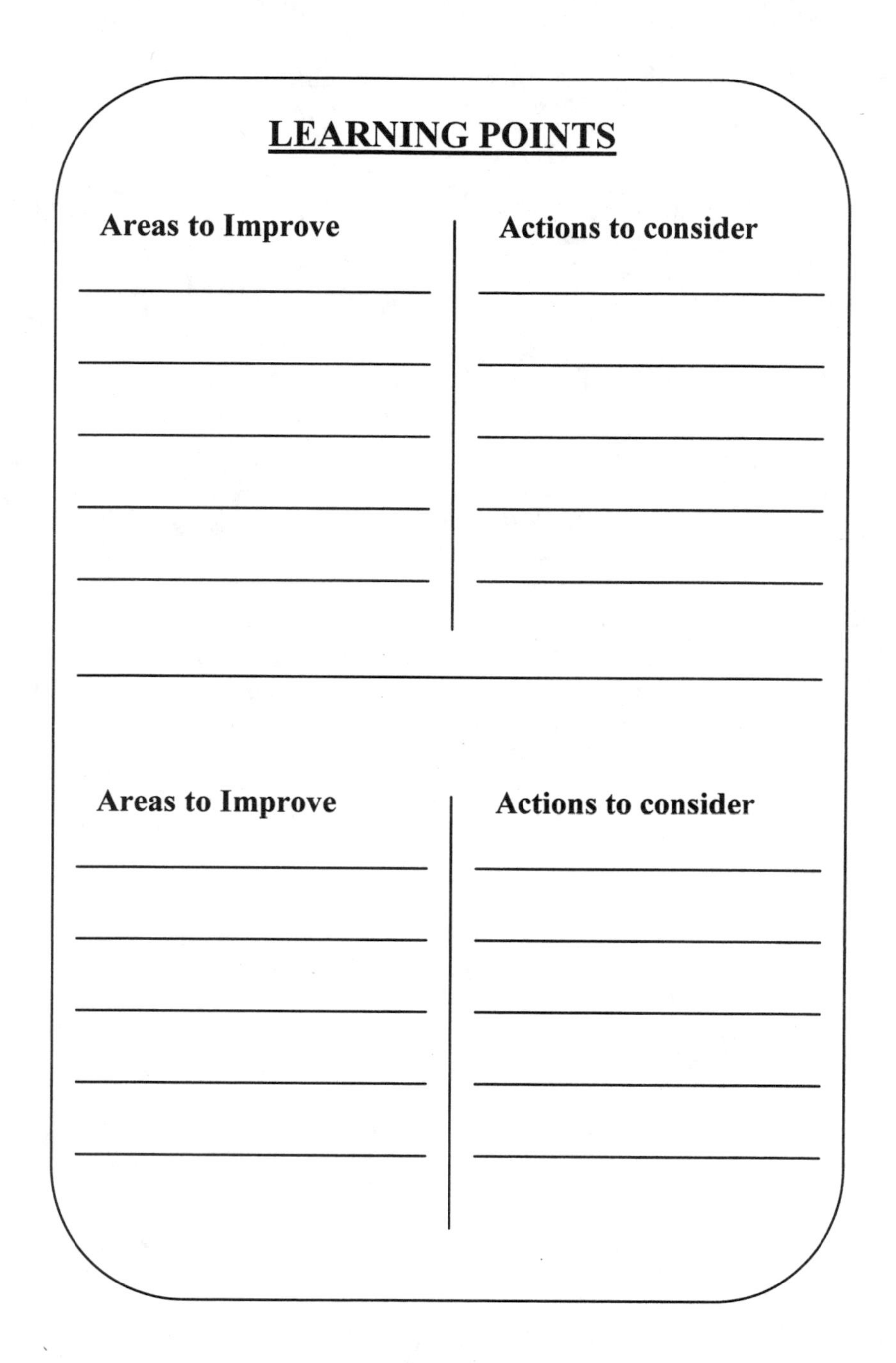
LEARNING POINTS
Areas to Improve
Actions to consider
Areas to Improve
Actions to consider

CHAPTER 13

CONCLUSION

My final recommendations for evolving in this profession.

This job is anything but boring. It entails so many different responsibilities and duties that one can never be bored with it. However, for experienced Administrative Assistants who have been on the job for a long time, there comes a time when you need to re-assess your responsibilities and how your work is done in order to find ways to improve your performance.

A good way of doing so is to look at how each portion of your work is done, write the process for each task on your job description. By reviewing your job description, you may be able to find that your job has evolved and some of your responsibilities can be eliminated, transferred to another department or to someone who reports to you. Perhaps you can take on more challenging responsibilities along the way.

In the meanwhile, I hope this book has been insightful and provided you with some tools and ideas to improve your professional and personal life. In conclusion, my personal recommendations for personal and professional growth are:

1. Be yourself: each one of us is an original. You come as a package and that package has many different facets, but it's still one package "You"

2. Be professional: your reputation will always follow you wherever you go

3. Be the "go to" person: serving as a reference point will make you someone who has longevity on the job and you will enjoy great fellowship among your co-workers

4. Do not gossip: if you are serious enough, people will not compromise you. Just by being a spectator, you can be a participant in gossips. Refute gossiping and let that be your reputation. People will not involve you when they are gossiping if you have the reputation of refusing to participate in gossiping

5. Get educated: advance your career through education. In this day and age, hard work is sometimes not enough. Management wants to know that you have the methodology and degrees to back your efforts. It can lead to promotions if your company promotes from within

6. Be organized: it will save you time, enhance the way you are perceived and be a great asset for your work ethics

7. Create a professional environment by behaving professionally. People will know you and refer to you as a professional. That's the reputation you want to follow you

8. Be ethical: don't get into any illegal activities on behalf of a boss, management or co-workers. You will also have to pay the price

9. Do it with a smile: keep a good attitude about work, even when you may not feel like it. Remember, you are not the only one who has to work

10. Be positive: don't whine even when you have too much work. Everybody loves a winner and nobody likes a whiner. If you have a positive attitude, you will project a positive image and will draw people to you. Remember you have to connect with others to be successful

11. Invest in something: the only way you will grow your money is by investing it. Just do it wisely and into something you have an interest in. Remember that you can always start small in whatever you invest in.

Good luck,
Justa

SURVIVAL GUIDE

FOR THE ADMINISTRATIVE ASSISTANT

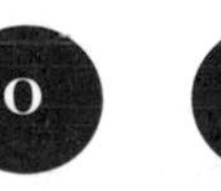

F O R M S

– I –

ORGANAZING FORMS

- Things To Do List – Monday To Friday
- Things To Do List – Full Week
- Things To Do List - Special

THINGS TO DO - WEEK OF: ____________

	MONDAY	TUESDAY	WEDNESDAY	THURSDAY	FRIDAY
8:00					
9:00					
10:00					
11:00					
12:00					
1:00					
2:00					
3:00					
4:00					
5:00					
6:00					

THINGS TO DO - WEEK OF: ____________

	MONDAY	TUESDAY	WEDNESDAY	THURSDAY	FRIDAY
8:00					
9:00					
10:00					
11:00					
12:00					
1:00					
2:00					
3:00					
4:00					
5:00					
6:00					

TO DO LIST - Week of: __________

MONDAY	TUESDAY	WEDNESDAY	THURSDAY	FRIDAY	SATURDAY	SUNDAY

CALLS	REMINDERS	BIRTHDAYS

– II –

MEETING ORGANIZATION

- Meeting Notice
- Agenda
- Sign-In Sheet
- Meeting Organizers - Contact List
- Meeting Participants - Contact List
- Meeting – To Do List
- Meeting Check List – Timeline

MARKETING MEETING NOTICE

FROM: Marketing Director

DISTRIBUTION:

Marketing Manager
Marketing Coordinator
CFO
COO
Engineering Manager

The next Marketing meeting will be held on:
Date: June 5, 2000,
Time: 9:00 a.m. - 12:00 p.m.

The meeting will take place at:
The Star Hotel
200 N. E. 25th Avenue
Somewhere Warm, CA 33333.

The purpose of the meeting is to present the new marketing plan for the new Excelsior 2000. Please confirm your availability by contacting Mary Nelson at 555-555-5555. Also, remember to send your items of discussion for the agenda.

Directions to the meeting:

MARKETING MEETING

FROM: Karen Jones - Marketing Director

LOCATION: Main Conference Room
Engineering, 3rd Floor

DATE & TIME: Thursday, September 06, 2007
9:00 – 11:00 a.m.

DISTRIBUTION:

Meeting Master
Marketing Manager
Marketing Coordinator
CFO
COO
Engineering Manager

AGENDA:

1. Minutes of the Meeting of (previous meeting date)
   1.1. Approve Minutes — Marketing Director
   1.2. Review Action Items — Meeting Director

2. Marketing Excelsior 2000 Project Update
   2.1. E-Commerce — Marketing Director
   2.2. Pay per Click — Marketing Coordinator
   2.3. Marketing Budget — CFO

3. Operations
   3.1. Site Location — COO
   3.2. Cost Evaluation — CFO
   3.3. Site Construction — Engineering Manager

4. Finance

5. Next Meeting

6. Adjournment

THE SIGN – IN SHEET

MEETING SIGN-IN SHEET Thursday, September 06, 2007		
1	Attendee Name	
2	Attendee Name	
3	Attendee Name	
4	Attendee Name	
5	Attendee Name	
6	Attendee Name	
7	Attendee Name	
8	Attendee Name	
9	Attendee Name	
10	Attendee Name	

MEETING CHECK LIST - TIMELINE

DATE	ITEM	DUTIES	✔
WEEKS PRIOR	MEETING LOCATION	Decide on location & reserve hotel if outside or reserve meeting room within company. Reconfirm every week and one day ahead of the meeting.	☐
	AGENDA	Start working on the agenda. Remember, it's a work in progress.	☐
	EQUIPMENT	If the meeting requires special equipment, reserve all equipment ahead of time.	☐
	PARTICIPANTS	Start creating the list of participants and create the contact sheet. Remember to confirm everyone.	☐
	FOOD	Create a menu and contact restaurant to order the food. Fax the food a week ahead of time and again confirm the day before.	☐
2 DAYS PRIOR	SHOPPING	There are many items that should be on hand at the meeting. Enclosed is list of shopping: Groceries: Napkins, Cups, Utensils Ice Drinks Water Office supplies: Pens Pads Markers Masking tape, Chart paper, etc.	☐
1 DAY PRIOR	THINGS TO BRING	Prepare a meeting packet, include: Sign in sheet, agenda (old & new), meeting hand-outs, table tents, extension cord, computer, contact sheet, old meeting minutes. Have two sets one for the meeting leader and one for you plus additional copies for all other participants. Save all documents on flash cards and carry with you	☐
	REMINDERS	Send email reminder to all participants Confirm meeting room & food	
DAY OF MEETING	MEETING ROOM	Arrive at least one hour prior to meeting time. Ensure all equipment if functional at least one hour prior to start of meeting. Set up tables & food & drink table Ensure audio-visual is operating	☐

MEETING ORGANIZERS
CONTACT LIST

ROLE	NAME	TEL	CELL	EMAIL
Meeting Manager				
Location Contact				
Caterer/Food				
Equipment				
Audio Visual				
IT Set Up Crew				

MEETING PARTICIPANTS - CONTACT LIST

NAME	TELEPHONE	CELL	EMAIL

MEETING "TITLE" – TO DO LIST
DATE & TIME OF MEETING

ITEM	WHAT TO DO	CONTACT	TEL	✔
LOCATION	Reserve location: contact person in charge of meeting room. Obtain firm confirmation. If outside, must have receipt or confirmation.			☐
MEETING MANAGER	Name of meeting Manager(s)			☐
PARTICIPANTS	Create list of participants, print and attach to this document. Include their emails and office and cellular phone numbers.			☐
MEETING DOCUMENT FOLDER	Create a meeting folder to keep all documents related to the meeting in that folder. What should be in that folder: agenda, previous agenda and minutes, sign-in sheet, menu from caterer, meeting attendant contact list with their telephone and cellular phone numbers			☐
AGENDA	The making of the agenda: What is the title of the meeting? Use any previous agenda as a guideline. Directors, managers and other interested parties will provide agenda items to be included on the agenda via e-mail, by phone or in person. Keep the information in the meeting folder.			☐
INVITATIONS	• Send invitations to all participants. • Request that they confirm. • Keep a list of all those who confirm. • If a participant hasn't confirmed, contact that person.			☐
EQUIPMENT	• Computer • Overhead projector & screen or flip chart • Audio visual equipment • High Intensity Overhead (Can Be Used As A Back-Up) • Conference phone & microphones • Extension cord & computer hook-ups • Internet Access Or Wireless			☐
SIGN-IN SHEET	As people are moved, the list must be updated to reflect the removal of those gone and the addition of newcomers.			☐
MEETING MATERIALS	• Meeting packet containing: agenda & attachments, minutes of previous meeting, sign-in sheet, table tents, business cards • Office supplies: pens, markers, masking tape, chart paper, etc.			☐
LOCATION/ LUNCH	With meeting manager, decide on type of food to be served. Plan a menu and ideas for lunch if you are serving lunch Remember to keep or bring:			☐
MEETING SET-UP	Ensure the room is properly set up with all necessary equipment for the meeting at least one hour prior to meeting start.			☐

– III –

CUSTOMER SERVICE

- Customer Service Form
- Customer Service Representative
- Customer Service - Job description

CUSTOMER SERVICE COMPLAINT FORM

By: ____________________

Client Information

Name:	Company:
Address:	City, State, Zip:
Office Tel:	Cellular:
Email:	Date and time:

Details of complaint or reason for call

Characteristics of Complaint

Product/Service:	Department:
Location:	

Resolution of complaint - Steps taken to resolve problem

Department or unit responsible for quality improvement notified: Yes □ No □
Product or service is replaced: Yes □ No □ Dollar Amount: $ ______________
Client is offered additional complimentary product or service: Yes □ No □
Is a survey completed to confirm level of satisfaction of resolution: Yes □ No □
Is a follow-up call or letter required: Yes □ No □

Customer Service
Job Description

- Answer the phone
- Receive client calls
- Process customer requests
- Investigate client complaints
- Follow up on client complaints
- Produce report of client complaints and copy all concerned parties/departments
- Remain current about products and services offered
- Make courtesy calls to the customers
- Keep a log of telephone calls received
- Keep a log of telephone calls issued, document the conversation and make an appointment on agenda of next date to call customer
- Communicate customer service issues to the other departments
- Maintain customer files and update contact name, address, telephone number and keep database current
- Maintain and update customer service procedure manual
- Report account inactivity of major accounts to the customer service supervisor.

– IV –

TECHNOLOGY AND YOU

- Microsoft Word – Shortcuts I
- Microsoft Word – Shortcuts II
- Microsoft Outlook – Shortcuts

MICROSOFT WINDOWS SHORTCUTS

ACTION	KEYS
Bold	CTRL – B
Copy	CTRL + C
Fonts	CTRL + D
Italics	CTRL + I
Launch Help	Windows Key F1
Paste	CTRL + V
Print	CTRL + P
Redo	CTRL + Y
Save	CTRL + S
Select All Items	CTRL + A
Spell Check	F7
Underline	CTRL + U
Undo	CTRL + Z
When In Doubt	Esc = Escape
Font Size To Normal	CTRL + Shift + N
Open A Document	CTRL + O
Close Window	CTRL + F4
Alignment Right	CTRL + R

Quick Key Strokes - Press SHIFT+ Any Of The Following Keystrokes To Select Text

ACTION	KEYS
LEFT ARROW	Left one character at a time
RIGHT ARROW	Right one character at a time
DOWN ARROW	Down one line at a time
UP ARROW	Up one line at a time
CTRL+ LEFT ARROW	Left one word at a time
CTRL+ RIGHT ARROW	Right one word at a time
HOME	To the beginning of the current line of text
END	To the end of the current line of text
CTRL+HOME	To the beginning of the document
CTRL+END	To the end of the document
PAGE UP	Up one full screen
PAGE DOWN	Down one full screen
CTRL+PAGE UP	To the beginning of the previous page
CTRL+PAGE DOWN	To the beginning of the next page

MICROSOFT OUTLOOK SHORTCUTS

ACTION	KEYS
Create Email	CTRL – Shift - M
Reply to Selected Email	CTRL – R
Forward Selected Email	CTRL – F
Save Draft of Email	CTRL – S
Create Flag or Follow-Up	CTRL – Shift – G
Create Contact	CTRL – Shift – C
Open Address Book	CTRL – Shift – B
Create Task	CTRL – Shift – K
Assign Task Category	Alt – G
Save and Close Task	Alt – S
Create Appointment	CTRL – Shift – A
Create Meeting Request	CTRL – Shift – Q
Create Note	CTRL – Shift – N
Open Selected Item	Enter
Close Window	Esc = Escape

– V –

LOOKING FOR WORK

- How To Create A Resume
- Resume Form
- Resume Samples
- Cover Letter Samples
- Thank You Letter
- Job Search Follow-Up Sheet
- How To Prepare A Job Description Preparation
- Sample Job Description

Go to www.Microsoft.com, search for templates. You will find a multitude of templates for professional resumes for various professions. You can also search on google.com, monster.com for advice on how to customize your resume.

HOW TO CREATE A RESUME

The resume must contain

Your personal information:

- Your name: in bigger font than anything else on the resume
- Address: residence or mailing
- Telephone: your cellular and home phone. If you don't have a phone, someone's phone where you can be reached
- Email: If you have a funny email like "sexygirl69@whatever.com," it is recommended that a more professional email containing your first or last name be created on Gmail, Hotmail, Yahoo, AOL, etc.

Career Goals or Professional Objective:

- A brief summary of your wish list, or expectations, for a position

Skills:

- A segment about your special skills. Include your computer skills and your level of computer literacy (if you have a Microsoft Office User Specialist (MOUS) certification provide the details of the certification,) numbers of words typed per minute WPM, special accomplishments, any languages written and/or spoken, internships, fellowships, military service, etc. Many employers value individuals from the military because of their training and work ethics

Education:

- Your education: starting with your most recent graduation or certification

Employment History:

- Start with your current or most recent position.
- Each position should be bullet pointed starting with the "From Date" to "End Date," name of company and your title

References:

- Available, or furnished, on request.

RESUME FORM

Your personal information:

Name: ______________________________

Address: ______________________________

City, State, Zip: ______________________________

Tel: ______________________________

Career Goals or Professional Objective:

____

____

Skills:

____

____

____

Employment History:

From: To: Company Name City, State

____

____

____

Education:

From: To: School Name City, State

____

____

References: ______________________________

123 Somewhere Street,
Warm City, CA 92000

Phone: (555) 555-5555
Email:MRobinson@Yahoo.com

Mary Robinson

Objective

Obtain an Executive Administrative Assistant position that will allow me to use my skills and further expand my career.

Skills Summary

Advance knowledge of the Microsoft Office Suite including: Word, Excel, Powerpoint and Outlook. Typing speed: 80 wpm. Languages: Fluent in: English, and some Spanish.

Experience

2004 – Present Pharmaco Company Fort Lauderdale, FL

Executive Administrative Assistant

- Prepared various reports under the supervision of the CEO
- Managed the CEO's schedule and coordinate his appointments
- Created and edited various spreadsheets for budgets
- Organized, planned and attended meetings.

2000–2004 Smith & Company Fort Lauderdale, FL

Administrative Assistant

- Created reports for the sales department.
- Provided support to the sales staff and management.
- Communicated with clients, mailed flyers and other promotional materials to clients.

1995–2000 Duffy Vineyards Fort Lauderdale, FL

Sales Support

- Created reports for the sales department.
- Provided support to the sales staff and management.
- Communicated with clients, mailed flyers and other promotional materials to clients.

Education

1991–1995 Broward Community College, Fort Lauderdale, FL

- Computer Science

References

Provided upon request.

MARY ROBINSON
7700 N. Hope Avenue
Beautiful City, FL 33333
Tel: (555) 555-1212
Email: MRobinson@msn.com

October 12, 2007

Jane Colins
Kolin-Werner
5200 W. Hire Street
Beautiful City, FL 33334

Reference: Executive Assistant Position

Dear Ms. Colins:

I am presenting my interest in the position mentioned above. I am a very experienced Executive Assistant with a strong background in successful business management support. I have worked in a broad range of professional and administrative positions and would welcome the opportunity to contribute to your organization. I should add that I have outstanding customer service qualifications.

My resume is enclosed for your review. Enclosed are a few points worth mentioning:

- Extensive experience with major accounts providing high-level support, building relationships and attending these important customers' needs.
- Excellent organizational, time-management planning and scheduling with the ability to adapt to schedule changes.
- Exceptional meeting on and off-site meeting management and organization.
- Above average knowledge of the Microsoft Office Suite including Outlook, Word, Excel, Powerpoint and Access database.

I am sure that I have all the skills required for this position and meet the goals of your company. I would appreciate the opportunity to meet you to discuss our mutual goals. I thank you in advance for your cooperation. Of course, you may contact me at any time at (555) 555-1212. Thank you for your consideration.

Sincerely,

Mary Robinson

MARY SMITH
7700 N. Hope Avenue
Beautiful City, FL 33333
Tel: (555) 555-1212
Email: MarySmith@yahoo.com

October 12, 2005

Ms. Jane Keller
Kolin-Werner
5200 W. Hire Street
Beautiful City, FL 33334

Reference: Position of Administrative Assistant

Dear Ms. Keller:

I am actively seeking a position as an executive assistant in a fast-paced and growing company. My five years of executive experience at Kolin-Werner have equipped me with a host of skills. With that said, I am very interested in the position and wish to continue my career with Meritas Laboratories.

Throughout my career I have demonstrated for my employers an exceptional facility for meeting organizational objectives and demands. In addition to my secretarial skills:

- I have advanced knowledge of the Microsoft Office Suite including: Word, Excel, Outlook and PowerPoint presentations.
- I am an excellent meeting organizer and have organized various meetings on-site and off-site. I also manage the meeting minutes drafting and distribution.
- Aside from the meetings, I am an adept event planner, having served as the director of the Kolin-Werner Christmas Ball for the last two years.
- My exceptional computer skills and meeting and event organization skills have proven useful for many of my employers.

I am certain I would prove to be an asset at Meritas Laboratories as well. If my abilities meet the needs of Meritas Laboratories, I would greatly appreciate the opportunity of speaking with you personally at your earliest convenience. Thank you for your time. I can be reached at (555) 555-1212.

Respectfully,

Mary Smith

MARY SMITH
7700 N. Hope Avenue
Beautiful City, FL 33333
Tel: (555) 555-1212
Email: MarySmith@yahoo.com

October 12, 2005

Ms. Jane Keller
Kolin-Werner
5200 W. Hire Street
Beautiful City, FL 33334

Reference: Position of Administrative Assistant

Dear Ms. Keller:

The purpose of this letter is to thank you for your time and your kindness during my recent interview with your company. I hope I have convinced you that I am the best candidate for the position. I am very excited about the possibility of becoming part of your team and hope that you have chosen me to be a part of your organization.

Should you need to communicate with me, you can reach me at (954) 555-1212.

Sincerely,

Mary Smith

JOB SEARCH FOLLOW-UP SHEET

JOB PROSPECT	
Job Title:	HR Contact:
Company Name:	Tel:
Product/Service offered:	Date sent:
Address:	Cover letter sent
City, State, Zip:	Email F/U sent:
Email Address:	Ad found in:
Thank You Note sent:	
Notes:	

JOB PROSPECT	
Job Title:	HR Contact:
Company Name:	Tel:
Product/Service offered:	Date sent:
Address:	Cover letter sent
City, State, Zip:	Email F/U sent:
Email Address:	Ad found in:
Thank You Note sent:	
Notes:	

HOW TO PREPARE A JOB DESCRIPTION

Your job description is simply a summary of your daily, weekly and monthly activities divided into specific categories. Ever wonder where the day has gone? A good way to monitor how time is spent is to document the time consumed on your daily activities. Enclosed is a grid that can be used to tally your activities.

ACTIVITY	QTY	TIME
Number of calls received		
Number of calls made		
Number of messages taken		
Letters/documents typed		
Photocopies		
Meetings scheduled		
Meeting attended (duration)		
Data entry or other typing		
Binding		
Report typing		
Order taking		
Document reviewing		

A job description should be as detailed as possible. It is a detailed outline of the work you perform as an employee and the responsibilities assigned to you or that you have taken the initiative for. If you are performing duties on a temporary basis, remember to add a section to include those duties. Do not hesitate to segment your job description. It is recommended that you have both a general job description and/or a partial job description. A condensed version of your job description will eventually become your resume.

SAMPLE JOB DESCRIPTION

Customer Service
Job Description

- Answer the phone
- Receive client calls
- Process customer requests
- Investigate client complaints
- Follow up on client complaints
- Produce report of client complaints and copy all concerned parties/departments
- Remain current about products and services offered
- Make courtesy calls to the customers
- Keep a log of telephone calls received
- Keep a log of telephone calls issued, document the conversation and make an appointment on agenda of next date to call customer
- Communicate customer service issues to the other departments
- Maintain customer files and update contact name, address, telephone number and keep database current
- Maintain and update customer service procedure manual
- Report account inactivity of major accounts to the customer service supervisor.

- VI -

HR FORMS/ORIENTATION

- Preparing For The Employee
- Human Resources Department Orientation – To Do List
- When The New Employee Starts – Items To Review And Training
- HR Forms – Yearly Goals
- HR Forms – Annual Review

COMPANY ORIENTATION

After the decision is made to hire the new employee and the employee has accepted the offer, the department employees should be advised of the information about the new employee including:

ACTIVITY	NOTES
Name of the new employee	
Who the new employee replaces	
What will be new employee's job description	
Who will the new employee report to	

Before new staff member arrives the Human Resources Department should:

ACTIVITY	NOTES
Who will be the supervisor	
A job description	
Instructions for first day and week	
Time and location of employment	
Company policy for parking (if available)	
Company dress code	
Work schedule including lunch break and other breaks	
Inform MIS personnel of new employee so they can create email account and set up computer system for new worker	

When the new employee starts

ACTIVITY	NOTES
Meet with supervisor (and others as appropriate) for office orientation	
Meet with company Human Resources	
Tour the building and immediate area	
Introduce employee to department employees and any other employees that will have contact with the new recruit	
Review the "Policy & Procedures" manual given to the employee	
Review the job description as it applies to the position	
Review the benefits package including insurance, retirement plan, tuition reimbursement, etc.	
Paid holidays, vacation and sick time	
Explain evaluation timeline and process	
Office goals and objectives	
How to use the telephone	
How to answer the telephone	

ACTIVITY	NOTES
Prepare and set up work-space	
Meet with colleagues and support staff	
Office organization (files location and office supplies cabinet)	
Handling incoming and outgoing mail	
Storage for personal belongings	
Restrooms, cafeteria and or/kitchen areas	
Copy & fax machines: How to use them, codes for photocopiers and fax (if needed), refilling paper supply & policies about number of copies and making personal copies	
Travel and reimbursement (especially for business travelers)	
Company credit card – Application/Rules	
Paying bills, making deposits, transferring between accounts	
Complete all necessary paperwork	
Get company ID and/or security card (if required)	

ACTIVITY	NOTES
Get company parking permit (if appropriate)	
Meet with MIS personnel for computer assistance to create email account and set up computer system for new worker (if not done yet)	
Hardware: turning on, backing up, printing, shutting down, etc.	
Software: systems used, company intranet, internet access, e-mail, etc. as needed	
Shutting down systems at the end of the day: lights, telephones, doors, computer, etc.	
Start the training	
Supervisor should not travel nor be absent for long periods at the beginning and should be available to answer questions.	

YEARLY PERFORMANCE GOALS

Employee Name:	Manager's Name:
Position/Title:	Department:

Employees: Please complete this form. Your supervisor and you will discuss the goals you developed for yourself, along with any goals he or she envisioned for you, and mutually agree on your Goals for the year. This will be done during the Performance Review Meeting.

Generally, there should be 3 to 5 Goals developed for the Year.

- **Goal statement** - Individual goals should support the growth and achievement of the business objectives.

  Goals must be:
  - **Specific**: explicitly define the goal
  - **Measurable**: delineate a way to quantify achievement of the goal
  - **Action-oriented**: achievement of the goal must require your doing something
  - **Realistic**: it must be possible to achieve the goal under current business conditions
  - **Time- and resource-constrained**: you should be able to delineate deadlines and budget.

- **Description** – provide information about:
  What is to be accomplished?
  Who will be involved?
  When the activity will be completed?
  How much will be used (in costs and resources)

- **Measurements** – Describe how you will measure the progress and results achieved.

Completed after the Employee and Manager have met and agreed on the Goals and the Goals stated above have been revised to reflect the agreed upon Goals:

Date Reviewed with Manager: ________________________

________________________ ________________________

Employee Manager

ANNUAL PERFORMANCE REVIEW

Review Period: ____________________

Review Date:______________________

Name of Employee:
Title:
Department:
Supervisor:

Employment Category:
Exempt ☐ Non-Exempt ☐

RATING SCALE

5–<u>OUTSTANDING</u>: Performance significantly exceeds the established job expectations. The employee consistently does outstanding work, regularly going far beyond what is expected of the employees in this job. Performance that exceeds expectations is due to the effort and skills of the employee.

4–<u>VERY GOOD</u>: Performance meets the established job expectations and in many instances, exceeds expectations. The employee is generally performing very well and requires little additional guidance.

3–<u>GOOD</u>: Performance may meet the established job expectations. The employee performs in a completely satisfactory manner and is performing at the level expected for employees in this position.

2–<u>NEEDS IMPROVEMENT</u>: Performance may meet some of the job expectations but does not fully meet the remainder. The employee generally is performing at a minimal level and improvement is needed to fully meet expectations. Performance deficiencies are due to the employee's lack of effort or skills.

1–UNSATISFACTORY: Performance generally fails to meet established expectations or requires frequent, close supervision and/or the redoing of work. The employee is not performing at the level expected for employees in this position. Unacceptable job performance is due to the employee's lack of effort or skills.

PRIMARY JOB RESPONSIBILITIES (Mirrors the Job Description Core Responsibilities)

Responsibility:

Employee Comments:

Supervisor Comments:

PERFORMANCE FACTORS	EMPLOYEE RATING	SUPERVISOR RATING
Knowledge of Work: Understands assigned duties and responsibilities; establishes priorities and plans work; uses appropriate procedures, tools, equipment and materials for assigned work.		
Quantity of Work: Work is complete, neat, accurate, timely and thoughtful. Completes all assignments within specified time limits; adjusts to unexpected changes in work demands to meet timetables.		
Initiative/Sense of Ownership: Self-starter requires minimal supervision, requests additional assignments or responsibilities; suggests and implements improved work methods. Takes ownership of problems and follows through until it is solved.		
Cooperation: Projects a positive work attitude; relates effectively with coworkers, supervisors, and others; uses tact and diplomacy/ acts professionally at all times.		
Problem Solving: Identifies problems, secures relevant information and implements solutions.		
Planning and Organizing: Establishes and manages work priorities; efficiently allocates time and utilizes available resources appropriately; effectively handles multiple assignments.		
Communications: Effectively expresses self in individual or group situations; message is clear, concise and easily understood; listens carefully to others.		
Attendance/Punctuality: Dependable, present at work and on time. (Approved leaves are not counted.)		

EMPLOYEES WITH SUPERVISORY RESPONSIBILITIES	EMPLOYEE RATING	SUPERVISOR RATING
Leadership: Effectively accomplishes work through others; inspires confidence, provides clear direction, communicates constructive feedback, provides on-the-job training; recognizes and resolves problems.		
Development of Staff: Recognizes and develops skills and abilities of other staff or students in order to promote professional development and to meet departmental and university objectives; plans and assigns work effectively and equitably.		

GOALS AND OBJECTIVES (Based on Annual Goals)			
Goal/Objective/ Project/ Assignment	**Results Achieved**	**Results Achieved**	**Supervisor Rating**
1.			
2.			
3.			
4.			

CAREER DEVELOPMENT PLAN (RECOMMENDED)		
Proposed Training, Education, or Experience	**Resources/Support Needed**	**Target Date**
OVERALL RATING JOB RESPONSIBILITIES & PERFORMANCE FACTORS AND GOALS & OBJECTIVES		

EMPLOYEE'S OVERALL RATING COMMENTS:	SUPERVISOR'S OVERALL RATING COMMENTS:

Your signature indicates only that you have read and discussed this performance review with your supervisor. It does not necessarily mean that you agree with the comments. If you disagree with your review, explain, either in the space above or on a separate page, the specific areas of disagreement.

I have reviewed the employee's job description:

☐ It is accurate and up-to-date; or

☐ It needs revisions – which is my responsibility.

☐ By checking the Box, I certify that a Midyear Review (of both Performance and Goals) was conducted with the employee during the year.

______________________	______________________
Employee Signature	**Date**
______________________	______________________
Supervisor Signature	**Date**

I have reviewed this evaluation:

______________________	______________________
Supervisor's Manager's Signature	**Date**

REAL ESTATE:
BONUS FORMS & LETTERS

– VII –

REAL STATE FORMS BUYERS & SELLERS

- Buyer Profile – Preliminary
- Buyers' Wish & Miss List
- Buyer Profile to manage a real estate transaction
- Request for Payoff
- Client Authorization For Payoff Request

BUYER PROFILE

Client Information: **Date:**

Name:	Cell:
Address:	Home:
City, State, Zip:	Work:
Email address:	Referred by:
SS:	DOB:

Property Description	
Location:	Type: House ▯ Condo ▯ Townhouse ▯ Duplex ▯ Efficiency ▯
Price Range: $	Pool: Yes ▯ No ▯
Rooms/Bathrooms:	Year Built:
Garage	Waterfront/Lakefront: Yes ▯ No ▯

Special Features Required:

Additional Notes:

SELLER'S INFO - LISTING

Client Information: **Date:**

Name:	Cell:
Address:	Home:
City, State, Zip:	Work:
Email address:	Referred by:

Property Description	
Location:	Type: House ▯ Condo ▯ Townhouse ▯ Duplex ▯ Efficiency ▯
Price: $	Pool: Yes ▯ No ▯
Rooms/Bathrooms:	Year Built:
Garage:	Waterfront/Lakefront: Yes ▯ No ▯
# of stories:	Sq Ft:
Land:	Other:

Community - Association

Legal Address:	Community Name
Fees: Association 1: Association 2:	Ammenities: Pool ▯ Club House ▯ Tennis ▯ Security ▯ Guard gate ▯ HOPA ▯ Other:
Contact:	Tel:

Additional Notes:

Special Features that attracted the seller originally to the house:

CLIENT WISH & MISS LIST
Property address
(Used when showing properties)

PREFERRED FEATURES	DISLIKES/ MISSING FEATURES

PERSONAL NOTES

CLOSING TRANSACTION FORM

Client Information	
Name:	Cell:
Address:	Home:
City, State, Zip:	Work:
Email address:	Referred by:
SS:	DOB:

Property Description	
Location:	Type: House ▯ Condo ▯ Townhouse ▯ Duplex ▯ Efficiency ▯
Price Range:	Pool: Yes ▯ No ▯
Rooms/Bathrooms:	Year Built:
Garage	Waterfront/Lakefront: Yes ▯ No ▯

Financing		
Closing Costs:	Credit Scores:	Equifax:
Down Payment:	Experian:	Transunion:
Bank:	Bank Info:	
Mortgage broker:	Tel:	Fax:
Mortgage Company:	Address:	

Conditions/Documents required	
Bank Statements:	Loan Application:
Mortgage Statement:	

Appraisal	
Name of Appraiser:	Tel:
Company:	Cost of Appraisal:

Title Company	
Company:	Tel:
Title Agent:	Fax:
Documents Required	
Recorded Warranty Deed	Recorded Warranty Deed
Proof of Hazard Insurance	Survey:
Proof of flood Insurance	Prior Title Insurance:
Homeowner' association's Contact	HOA – Payment

Include Logo Of Listing Real Estate Company
Address, City, State and Zip
Telephone & Fax

CONTACT INFORMATION FOR LISTING

ENTITY	NAME	CONTACT INFO
PROPERTY ADDRESS		
SELLER'S INFORMATION		
LISTING AGENT		
BUYER'S INFORMATION		
BUYER'S AGENT		
MANAGEMENT OFFICE		
MORTGAGE COPANY		
TITLE COMPANY		
INSPECTION		
APPRAISAL		

Title Company – Logo if available or use company letterhead
Full Address, including suite #
City, State, Zip
Telephone: (555) 555-5550
Facsimile: (555) 555-5555

Date:____________________

Company: ___________________________

Attn: PAYOFF DEPARTMENT

Fax: ______________________________

Re: Borrower: *Name*
Property Address: *Full Address*
City, State, Zip

SS# ***-**-*9999*
Loan #: _______________

Please provide this office your statement of the balance due relative to the above account GOOD THRU *Date*: __________.

This transaction contemplates that your account is to be satisfied at closing. Would you please fax your statement, to our office at *(555) 555-5555*.

Your prompt attention in supplying the necessary information is greatly appreciated.

Sincerely,

Jane Doe

CLIENT AUTHORIZATION FOR PAYOFF REQUEST

Closing Coordinator

I, ___________________(name of client), authorize Title Company to obtain the payoff information in reference to the above mentioned loan. Please fax the payoff to (555) 555-5555. If you have any questions, please do not hesitate to contact me.

____
SIGNATURE OF CLIENT

– VIII –

REAL ESTATE FORMS - RENTALS

- Rental Application
- Rental Verification
- Payment coupons (used to mail payments monthly)
- Rental Payment Statement
- Rental Contact Info – For both Owner and Renters when exchanging documents

RENTAL APPLICATION

Date:

Applicant Information	
Name:	Cell:
Current Address:	
City, State, Zip:	Work:
How Long?	Home:
Owned ☐ Rented ☐	Monthly Payments:
SS:	DOB:
Previous Address:	
City, State, Zip:	

Employment Information	
1) Current Employer & Supervisor:	
Employer Address:	Tel:
City, State, Zip:	How Long?
2) Previous Employer & Supervisor:	
Employer Address:	Tel:
City, State, Zip:	How Long?

RENTAL APPLICATION CONT'D

References	
1- Name:	Tel:
Address:	
City, State, Zip:	How Long?
2 - Name:	Tel:
Address:	
City, State, Zip:	How Long?
3 - Name:	Tel:
Address:	
City, State, Zip:	How Long?

I authorize the verification of the information provided on his form as to my credit and employment, reference for myself and for my corporation. I have received a copy of this application.

______________________________ ____________________

Signature of Applicant Date

RENTAL VERIFICATION FORM

The purpose of this verification is to obtain reference from previous renters and to report the rental payment activities to the credit bureaus if applicable.

APPLICANT INFORMATION

Name of Applicant (s):	
Social Security Number(s):	
Address of Property:	
Dates of Residency:	From: To:
Amount of Rent	$
Has Lease Expired?	YES ☐ NO: ☐
# of Late or NSF's	None ☐ 1 ☐ 2☐ 3☐ 4+ ☐
If 4 or more, did they occur within the last twelve months?	YES ☐ NO: ☐
Has the individual complied with all community policies?	YES ☐ NO: ☐
Does this individual keep an animal on the premises?	YES ☐ NO: ☐
Has the animal at any time caused a problem or been a nuisance?	YES ☐ NO: ☐
Is this individual Eligible for re-rental?	YES ☐ NO: ☐

OWNER/MANAGER INFORMATION

Name of owner/Manager:	
Name of Company/Address:	
Contact Information - Tel:	

______________________ Date ______________________

Authorized Owner/
Manager's Signature

Company – Logo if available or use company letterhead
Full Address, including suite #
City, State, Zip
Telephone: (555) 555-5550
Facsimile: (555) 555-5555

CONTACT INFORMATION FOR RENTAL
Enclose Full Address of Property Rented
Form Given With Rental Package To New Renter

ENTITY	NAME	CONTACT INFO
PROPERTY OWNER		
PROPERTY RENTER		
MANAGEMENT OFFICE		
LISTING AGENT		
RENTER'S AGENT		
ELECTRICAL COMPANY		
WATER/UTILITY COMPANY		

PAYMENT COUPONS FOR RENTAL PROPERTIES

These coupons are used to mail rental payments to the property owner. They are especially important when the owner has multiple rental properties. This coupon is an excellent source of identification of which renter is sending payment.

PAYMENT COUPON

Lessor:
Name of Owner
Address of Owner
City, State, Zip
Telephone of Owner

Lessee:
Name of Renter
Address of Property Rented
City, State, Zip

Payment for month of: ____________________

Amount: ____ **$2000.00**

After the 6th of the month, include the late fee for a total amount of: ***$2050.00***

Name of Property owner-Lessor
Address
City, State, Zip

RENTAL PAYMENT STATEMENT

Name of Renter - Lessee
Address of renter
City, State and Zip

Emergency Contact Information
Name Of Owner
Tel: of Owner (555) 222-3333

Lease Information

Total Rent Due 01/01/2006 –
Pay: **$1200**
(amount of rent)

After the 07/06/2006 –
Pay $30 late fee: **$1230**
(amount of rent incl. late fee)

Lease Term: Yearly
From: 01/01/2007
To: 12/31/2007

– IX –

REAL ESTATE FORMS - HOA

- Condo Documents Delivery Confirmation
- Homeowner's Association Document Delivery Notice
- Sample letter to submit to HOA for prospective clients

Include Logo Of Listing Real Estate Company
Address, City, State and Zip
Telephone & Fax

CONDO DOCUMENTS DELIVERY CONFIRMATION

Condominium Association Rules & Regulations Document delivered to:

Name of Company:	Buyer's Agent Real Estate Company
Client:	______________________________
Name of Recipient:	______________________________
Signature of Recipient:	______________________________
Date Delivered:	______________________________
For Realtor:	Name of buyer's agent

NOTE: *Client has three (3) days to review the condo documents. If client is not accepted, client must return the documents to: (include name of listing real estate company). Attn: (name of realtor). If documents are not returned, a copy will be purchased from the association and billed to (real estate representing buyer who kept copy of condo documents).*

Include Logo Of Real Estate Company
Address, City, State and Zip
Telephone & Fax

Date: ________________

Name of agent processing application
Name of Association
Address,
City, State and Zip

Reference: Application for sale or lease at the (give name of Community) some associations manage multiple communities For: (give clients' names)

Dear __________:

Please find enclosed an application for prospective owner(s)/tennant(s) for the property located at (give full address of property). State the name of the current owners and their agreement to sell/rent the property to the prospective owner(s)/tennant(s).

Present the family with the names of individual(s) if it's a family, name the spouses, children or any other parties who will live with them. Provide the association with a history of the family, their employment situation, etc.

List of the required documents that you are submitting:

- Check for association application fee (very important)
- A copy of the sales contract or lease/agreement to enter into a lease
- Copies of ID, driver's license, etc.
- Pet registration (if applicable)
- Police reports and list of references if required

Ensure that the application is complete before submitting to the application or it will delay the process. Thank the person who will process the application in advance for your cooperation. You can reach me at (555) 222-5555.

Yours truly,
Buyer's Agent Signature

INDEX

INDEX

INDEX

INDEX